Echoes of the Highlands: The Story of the Scottish People

Echoes of the Highlands: The Story of the Scottish People

Francis Williams

Echoes of the Highlands: The Story of the Scottish People

Copyright © 2025 by Francis Williams

All rights reserved. No part of this publication may be reproduced, distributed, or transmitted in any form or by any means, including photocopying, recording, or other electronic or mechanical methods, without the prior written permission of the publisher, except in the case of brief quotations embodied in critical reviews and certain other noncommercial uses permitted by copyright law.

First Edition: 2025

ISBN: 978-1-997668-44-2

Cover design by The Author
Printed in USA

Disclaimer: The information in this book is provided for general educational purposes only. Please see full disclaimer.

For Eilidh and Zahra,

May Love, Peace and Joy

Accompany You Always

September 5th 2025

"May the road rise up to meet you,
May the wind be always at your back.
May the sun shine warm upon your face,
The rains fall soft upon your fields,
And until we meet again,
May God hold you in the palm of His hand."

Echoes of the Highlands: The Story of the Scottish People

Table of Contents

Introduction 1

Chapter 2: Picts, Gaels, and Norsemen: A Cultural Tapestry 7

Chapter 3: Forging a Kingdom: From Alba to Scotland 11

Chapter 4: The Wars for Freedom: Wallace, Bruce, and the Fight for Independence 17

Chapter 5: Clans and Castles: The Heartbeat of Highland Life 23

Chapter 6: The Reformation and the Rise of the Kirk 29

Chapter 7: Crowns United: A Tale of Two Kingdoms 35

Chapter 8: Enlightenment and the Age of Ideas 41

Chapter 9: From Crofts to Coal: The Industrial Transformation 47

Chapter 10: Tartan, Bagpipes, and Myths: The Cultural Soul of Scotland 53

Chapter 11: Across the Seas: The Scottish Diaspora 59

Chapter 12: Scotland and the Empire: Partners and Paradoxes 65

Chapter 13: The Spirit of Independence: From Arbroath to Holyrood 71

Chapter 14: The Makers: Great Scots Who Changed the World 77

Chapter 15: The Everlasting Flame: Scotland in the Modern World .. 83

Bibliography 89

Glossary 95

Timeline of Major Events 101

Disclaimer

This book is intended for general educational and entertainment purposes. While every effort has been made to ensure accuracy, the author and contributors do not claim that this work is exhaustive or free from error. Historical interpretation is a dynamic and evolving field, and new research may provide additional insights beyond what is presented here.

The author and publisher accept no responsibility for any errors, omissions, or consequences arising from the use of this book. Readers interested in in-depth study are encouraged to consult primary sources and scholarly works listed in the bibliography and further reading sections.

Acknowledgment of AI Tools

Portions of the research, editing, and structuring of this book were supported by advanced AI tools, including language models trained by OpenAI. These tools were used to help synthesize historical research, enhance narrative flow, and organize content in a clear and accessible manner.

Introduction

Scotland: a land of rugged highlands, misty glens, and deep, mysterious lochs. A place where the wind whispers ancient secrets through the stones of ruined castles and the waves crash upon cliffs that have watched over countless generations. The story of Scotland is not simply the story of a nation — it is a saga of a people whose spirit has endured wars, reformations, unions, and global migrations, leaving an imprint far beyond its windswept shores.

At first glance, Scotland might seem like a small corner of the British Isles, but its historical and cultural influence radiates across the world. The Scots have gifted humanity with some of its greatest thinkers, engineers, poets, and pioneers. Yet, to truly understand Scotland's contribution to the world, one must journey deep into its past, where myths intertwine with facts and where the roots of a resilient national character were planted.

The earliest chapters of this story begin with hunter-gatherers who roamed the forests and fished the coastal waters over 12,000 years ago. They left behind silent monuments: Neolithic tombs perfectly aligned with the solstice sun, stone circles that still stand like guardians of ancient mysteries, and village ruins revealing surprisingly sophisticated lifestyles. These early Scots were already shaping a unique identity, deeply tied to nature and the land.

As time moved forward, waves of different peoples—Picts, Gaels, Britons, Norsemen—crashed into each other, blending and clashing in equal measure. Each left a distinct mark on Scotland's cultural DNA. Their languages, art, and spiritual beliefs merged, creating a complex, layered identity that still resonates in place-names, folklore, and traditions today. In no other country is hybridity so clearly a source of strength rather than weakness.

Then came the forging of a kingdom, the unification under a single monarch, and the long, bitter struggle to defend that hard-won sovereignty. The Wars of Independence were more than battles; they were the crucible in which modern Scottish identity was formed. Figures like William Wallace and Robert the Bruce were not mere warriors but symbols of a collective yearning for freedom, echoing across the centuries to the present-day independence debates.

Religion, too, played its part. The Scottish Reformation did not simply reshape theology; it transformed society, education, and even politics. The rise of the Presbyterian Kirk gave Scotland a new sense of mission and community — a fierce belief in the right to self-governance under God's law rather than a king's whim.

Even as Scotland entered into a union with England and later into the British Empire, it retained a distinct cultural pulse. The Enlightenment saw Scots leading the world in philosophy and science, while the Industrial Revolution turned cities like Glasgow into global powerhouses of innovation and industry. However, this came at a cost: the clearances, poverty, and mass emigration, which created a Scottish diaspora that carried their homeland's spirit to every continent.

Today, echoes of the Scottish story can be heard in New Zealand's rolling hills, in Nova Scotia's fishing villages, and in the tartan parades of American cities. The global Scottish community continues to evolve, carrying forward a legacy of perseverance, creativity, and cultural pride.

In this book, we will wander through these valleys of history, climb the battlements of ancient castles, sit beside loch shores at dusk, and listen to the ballads that tell of love, loss, and resistance. We will meet saints and scholars, rebels and poets, engineers and dreamers. Through each chapter, we will piece together the tapestry of a people who have always seen themselves not just as subjects of a land, but as custodians of a timeless story.

So grab your walking stick, don your tartan, and follow me into the mists of time, where we will uncover the enduring soul of Scotland — a story as wild, beautiful, and indomitable as the land itself.

Chapter 1: Ancient Roots and Mystical Beginnings

Before the names of kings were inscribed in chronicles, before the clang of swords echoed through glens, and before the bagpipe's haunting call rolled across the heathered hills, there were the first peoples — those who laid the earliest foundations of Scotland's story.

Over 12,000 years ago, as the last great glaciers receded from northern Europe, small bands of hunter-gatherers made their way into what would become Scotland. These hardy souls tracked deer across dense forests, fished the rich coastal waters, and gathered roots and berries from meadows. Their lives were woven into the rhythms of nature, and though they left no written records, their presence can be felt in the ghostly silhouettes of ancient structures scattered across the landscape.

Among the most evocative of these ancient sites is Skara Brae, a Neolithic settlement on Orkney dating to around 3200 BC. Imagine a cluster of stone homes nestled together, each with stone beds, storage niches, and hearths where families would have gathered for warmth against the fierce North Sea winds. Covered passages connected the dwellings, suggesting a strong sense of community and mutual protection. These early Scots may have been primitive by today's standards, but their ingenuity and adaptability reveal a people deeply attuned to their harsh, beautiful environment.

Another marvel is Maes Howe, a stone-built tomb aligned so that, during the winter solstice, sunlight penetrates the passage and illuminates the central chamber. This architectural precision hints at a sophisticated understanding of astronomy and a spiritual connection to celestial cycles. Standing inside Maes Howe as the sun pierces the darkness is to share a moment with ancestors who saw the world as a place of spirits, mysteries, and sacred rhythms.

Scotland's landscape is dotted with stone circles, most famously the Ring of Brodgar, also on Orkney. Like Stonehenge in England, these circles may have been used for ceremonies, rituals, or gatherings that strengthened social bonds and reaffirmed connections to the natural and spiritual world. Each stone, weathered by millennia of wind and rain, stands as a silent witness to countless generations who have passed.

By around 700 BC, the Iron Age had arrived, bringing new technologies and social structures. Metalwork flourished, from intricate jewelry to deadly weapons, and Celtic knotwork began to adorn objects, symbolizing eternity and interconnectedness. Settlements expanded, hillforts rose across strategic high points, and trade networks reached far beyond the Scottish shores.

Among the ancient inhabitants were the mysterious Picts, known as the "painted people." Roman chroniclers, who first mentioned them in the late 3rd century AD, described fierce warriors who covered their bodies with elaborate tattoos or paint. The Picts left behind carved stones bearing enigmatic symbols — spirals, animals, warriors — whose meanings still baffle scholars today. Their art suggests a society rich in mythology and symbolism, a tapestry of stories etched in stone rather than parchment.

Parallel to the Picts were the Gaels, or Scots, who arrived from Ireland in the early centuries AD. They established the kingdom of Dál Riata in the western Highlands, forging strong maritime ties with their Irish homeland. Their culture emphasized kinship, oral storytelling, and a warrior ethos. The Gaels brought with them the Gaelic language, which would become a foundational element of Highland identity.

Meanwhile, the Britons inhabited the southern regions, speaking a language closely related to Welsh, and maintaining ties to their Celtic cousins in what is now Wales and Cornwall. The arrival of the Angles and Saxons from the south introduced further cultural complexity, as did the later Norse invasions, which left an indelible mark on the northern isles and coastal communities.

What emerges from this intricate web of migrations, conflicts, and alliances is a portrait of a land that was never culturally isolated but rather a vibrant crossroads. The names of places — Ben Nevis (Gaelic), Stornoway (Norse), Aberdeen (Pictish) — tell stories of diverse peoples intermingling, negotiating identities, and building a collective spirit.

Early spiritual life before Christianity centered around nature: sacred groves, springs imbued with spirits, and ancestral veneration. Kings of Dál Riata, for instance, were thought to descend from gods, and chieftains sought the blessings of druids before battle. These beliefs were not simply religion in a narrow sense; they were frameworks that bound communities together, offered explanations for the mysteries of life and death, and gave meaning to the cycles of the sun and moon.

In 563 AD, the Irish monk St. Columba sailed to the island of Iona, a place that would become the cradle of Scottish Christianity. Columba's mission to convert the Picts marked a new chapter — a gradual transformation of spiritual life that would ultimately unify disparate tribes under a shared faith, paving the way for political unification centuries later.

Yet, even as Christian crosses replaced ancient totems, echoes of the old ways lingered in folk traditions, seasonal festivals, and oral tales. The mythology of kelpies, selkies, and the Cailleach (the old hag goddess of winter) carried forward the deep bond with nature and the uncanny.

Looking back at these earliest chapters of Scottish history is to look into a mirror reflecting resilience, adaptability, and a profound connection to land and community. These qualities would become the foundation of Scottish identity, enduring through centuries of strife and change.

In the twilight of a Highland evening, when the sky burns with soft amber and purple hues and the wind rustles through the heather, one can almost hear the whispers of these ancient ancestors — calling us to remember that every stone, every loch, and every wild hill carries the memory of those who came before.

Chapter 2: Picts, Gaels, and Norsemen: A Cultural Tapestry

Imagine standing on a rugged Scottish hilltop at dawn. The mists slowly lift, revealing glens and lochs shimmering like silver in the early light. You hear whispers carried by the breeze — echoes of ancient peoples whose footsteps once pressed these same stones. These voices belong to the Picts, the Gaels, and the Norsemen, each a vital thread in the intricate tapestry of Scottish identity.

The Mysterious Picts: "Painted People" of the North

The Picts have long captured the imagination of historians and storytellers alike. Their name, derived from the Latin *Picti*, meaning "painted ones," hints at their fierce reputation and enigmatic customs. Roman writers described them as elusive warriors who vanished into the mist, striking fear into even the most disciplined legions.

Living in northern and eastern Scotland from the late Iron Age into the early medieval period, the Picts left behind few written records. Instead, they spoke through their carved stones — mysterious standing slabs adorned with cryptic symbols of beasts, intricate knots, and swirling designs. These stones stand scattered across the landscape like silent sentinels, guardians of secrets we are only beginning to decipher.

The Picts were skilled farmers and warriors, known for their hillforts and their tenacity in resisting Roman incursions. Despite repeated attempts, the Romans never fully conquered northern Scotland, which they labeled "Caledonia" — a land of wild mountains and wilder people. Instead, they built the mighty Hadrian's Wall and later the Antonine Wall to keep the "barbarians" at bay.

The Picts' culture was rich in mythology and oral storytelling. Tales were passed down from druid to child, teaching lessons about bravery, nature, and the unseen world. Their society celebrated artistry, as evidenced by their metalwork and jewelry, which often featured complex animal motifs and knotwork symbolizing eternity and interconnectedness.

Over time, the Picts began to merge culturally and politically with their neighbors, especially the Gaels. This blending marked the beginning of a new, unified Scottish identity — but the spirit of the Picts remains alive today in place names, folklore, and the enduring sense of mystery that hovers over the northern hills.

The Gaels: Seafarers and Kingdom Builders

While the Picts held the east and north, another powerful force arrived from across the sea: the Gaels, or Scots. Originating from Ireland, these adventurous seafarers crossed the stormy waters in the early medieval period to settle in the western Highlands and islands.

The Gaels established the kingdom of Dál Riata, with its heart in Argyll and the surrounding islands. They brought with them their Gaelic language, a lyrical tongue that would become the heartbeat of Highland poetry, music, and identity. Their bards wove stories of hero-kings, gods, and tragic love, planting seeds for a rich oral tradition that still thrives.

Life among the Gaels revolved around kinship and loyalty to clan and chieftain. A person's worth was deeply tied to their family ties and honor. They were fierce warriors but also skilled sailors and traders, navigating treacherous coastal waters with confidence. Their ships, called *currachs*, glided across the sea like dark spirits, linking Scotland to Ireland and beyond.

Religion among the Gaels before Christianization was deeply entwined with nature. They revered sacred groves, springs, and hilltops. Spirits and gods inhabited every rock and stream, and druidic ceremonies were central to their communal life. Seasonal festivals celebrated the rhythms of the earth — the sowing of seeds, the harvest, the solstice sun. These pagan traditions subtly survived even after Christianity arrived, living on in folk customs and seasonal celebrations.

The Gaels' encounter with the Picts led to centuries of conflict, alliances, and eventually a blending of cultures. By the mid-9th century, Kenneth MacAlpin, a king of Dál Riata, would famously unite the Picts and Gaels, founding the kingdom of Alba — the early name for Scotland. This unification set the stage for the emergence of a single, powerful nation.

The Norsemen: Raiders and Settlers from the North

As the Gaels and Picts were merging, new visitors began arriving from the north — the Norsemen, or Vikings. Starting in the late 8th century, these Scandinavian warriors first appeared as terrifying raiders, their longships slicing through misty seas, their axes and swords gleaming under gray skies.

Initially feared as plunderers, the Norsemen soon transitioned from mere raiders to settlers. They claimed the Orkney and Shetland islands, as well as parts of the northern mainland and the Hebrides. With them, they brought their own language, laws, and customs, which left a profound imprint on these regions.

Unlike the Gaels and Picts, the Norse saw the sea not as a barrier but as a highway. They connected Scotland to a wider Viking world stretching from Scandinavia to Iceland, Greenland, and even as far as North America. Their settlements on the Scottish islands became vital outposts for trade and exploration.

The Norse influence is still evident in place names today — Stornoway, Sumburgh, and Wick, to name a few. Norse mythology also merged with local beliefs, enriching the cultural tapestry with tales of sea monsters, shape-shifters, and hidden treasure. Even today, the Up Helly Aa festival in Shetland celebrates this Viking heritage, with fiery processions and the burning of a ceremonial longship lighting up the winter darkness.

Despite their fearsome reputation, the Norse integrated with local populations over time, intermarrying and adopting aspects of Pictish and Gaelic culture. By the later Middle Ages, many Norse territories would gradually come under Scottish control, but the legacy of their adventurous, seafaring spirit endures.

A Melting Pot of Peoples and Traditions

What makes Scotland's early medieval period so remarkable is the interplay of these different peoples — Picts, Gaels, and Norse — each adding their unique thread to the evolving national tapestry.

This confluence was not simply about battles and borders; it was a living, breathing process of cultural negotiation. Languages mixed, customs blended, and religious practices adapted. Over time, rather than erasing each other, these diverse strands wove together to form something distinctively Scottish.

The hybrid nature of Scotland's identity is still evident today. The resilience and independence of the Picts, the poetic soul and seafaring daring of the Gaels, and the adventurous, outward-looking spirit of the Norse continue to shape Scottish character. Together, they gave rise to a people deeply rooted in land and sea, fiercely proud yet open to the world beyond their shores.

As we move forward into the next chapters — from the formation of Alba to the Wars of Independence and beyond — we carry with us this foundation of cultural hybridity. It reminds us that Scotland has always been, at its heart, a place of meeting: of clans and kingdoms, of myths and histories, of ancient traditions and new ideas.

So when you next hear the wind sighing over the heather or see the northern lights flicker above the sea, remember that these are not just beautiful moments in nature. They are echoes of the Picts' painted warriors, the Gaels' sea-kings, and the Norse adventurers who together dreamed Scotland into being.

Chapter 3: Forging a Kingdom: From Alba to Scotland

By the ninth century, the rugged lands of what we now call Scotland were home to a rich tapestry of cultures — the mysterious Picts, the sea-faring Gaels, the sturdy Britons, and the adventurous Norse. But these diverse peoples were not content to remain mere neighbors; a new chapter was about to unfold — one that would bind them under a single crown and give rise to the kingdom of Scotland.

At the heart of this transformation was Kenneth MacAlpin, a figure who stands at the crossroads of myth and history. Kenneth, king of the Gaels of Dál Riata, is often credited with uniting the Picts and Scots around 843 AD. Though historians continue to debate the precise details — whether it was a peaceful inheritance or a forceful conquest — what matters most is the result: a new kingdom known as Alba.

The creation of Alba was not simply a merging of territories. It was a delicate weaving together of cultures, traditions, and rival ambitions. The Gaelic language began to spread more widely, gradually overtaking Pictish, which slowly faded into memory. The stories, beliefs, and social structures of the Picts did not vanish entirely, however. Instead, they became folded into the new Gaelic-led identity, creating a richer cultural fabric.

The Shaping of a Kingdom

As Alba took shape, its kings faced a monumental task: consolidating power across a land marked by deep forests, forbidding mountains, and isolated glens. Scotland's rugged geography — often an obstacle to would-be conquerors — also made internal unity a daunting challenge.

The early kings, including Kenneth's successors like Constantine II and Malcolm I, spent decades expanding their control over outlying regions. They pushed into former Pictish territories, forged alliances with the

Britons of Strathclyde, and watched warily as the Norse continued to press their claims on the northern and western isles.

One important step in defining the kingdom's territorial integrity was the annexation of Strathclyde in the early 11th century. The Britons of Strathclyde, centered around what is now Glasgow, had maintained their independence through centuries of strife. Their eventual integration marked a significant milestone, further broadening the kingdom's reach and diversifying its population.

Meanwhile, in the southeast, the Scottish kings set their sights on Lothian, then controlled by the Angles of Northumbria. By 1018, under King Malcolm II, Scotland had secured Lothian after the decisive Battle of Carham. This victory extended Scottish influence down to the River Tweed and established a border that remains largely intact today.

The Role of Christianity

While military campaigns and political marriages played crucial roles in unifying the kingdom, religion was perhaps an even stronger unifying force. Christianity had taken root centuries earlier with St. Columba's mission from Iona, but it was under the new kingdom of Alba that it became fully integrated into political life.

Monasteries blossomed across the land, becoming centers of learning, literacy, and political influence. The church helped legitimize royal authority, acting as a stabilizing force among restive nobles and warring clans. In many ways, the spread of Christianity mirrored the spread of the kingdom itself: slow, uneven, but ultimately transformative.

The abbey at Iona remained a spiritual heartland, a place where kings sought both divine favor and eternal rest. To be buried at Iona was not merely a sign of faith but a powerful symbol of legitimate kingship. Even today, walking among the weathered gravestones of Iona feels like stepping into the pulse of an ancient spiritual lineage.

Castles and Clans: The Fabric of Medieval Society

As the Scottish kingdom solidified, so too did its social structures. By the High Middle Ages, the landscape was increasingly dotted with castles — symbols of both defense and authority. These fortresses, built first in wood and later in imposing stone, projected power over the surrounding countryside and provided refuge during raids or rebellions.

The rise of castles also coincided with the emergence of the clan system, especially in the Highlands. Clans were extended kin groups united under a chief, bound by blood ties and shared loyalty. While often romanticized today, the reality of clan life was complex: a mixture of kinship solidarity, fierce rivalries, and constant negotiation over land and resources.

In the Lowlands, feudalism took deeper root, with powerful lords owing allegiance to the king and controlling vast estates. The interplay between Highland clan autonomy and Lowland feudal structures would later become a defining feature of Scottish politics and culture, sometimes causing friction but also contributing to Scotland's unique character.

External Threats and the Spark of National Identity

The forging of Scotland was not solely an inward-looking affair. Throughout this period, the looming threat from the south — England — played a critical role in shaping the kingdom's identity.

Relations with England were often tense and complicated. While periods of peace and strategic marriages occurred, conflicts over borders and sovereignty simmered persistently. These tensions would soon erupt into the epoch-defining Wars of Independence, but even before that, the need to present a united front against English ambitions was a strong motivator for internal consolidation.

The growing sense of being "Scottish" — distinct from English, Norse, or Irish — took shape slowly but powerfully during this period. While earlier identities had been rooted in tribe or region, the emergence of a shared monarchy, common religious institutions, and shared struggles fostered a collective national consciousness.

This budding national identity found symbolic expression in art, poetry, and chronicles written by monastic scribes. It was during this time that the legendary figure of Macbeth appeared — first as a historical king who ruled from 1040 to 1057, and later immortalized (and somewhat maligned) by Shakespeare. The real Macbeth was a competent ruler who made a pilgrimage to Rome, reflecting both the internal stability of his reign and Scotland's growing connection to the wider Christian world.

The Normans Arrive: A New Influence

In the 12th century, under kings like David I, Scotland underwent a new wave of transformation influenced by Norman culture. David had spent years in the English court and admired Norman administrative systems and military innovations. When he became king, he encouraged Norman nobles to settle in Scotland, granting them lands and titles in exchange for loyalty and service.

These new barons introduced stone castles, improved feudal structures, and continental legal traditions. Scottish towns began to grow around royal burghs, market centers that became engines of economic and social development. This period saw the foundation of many towns still vital today: Edinburgh, Perth, Stirling, and Aberdeen, among others.

The influence of Norman settlers helped modernize Scotland's governance but also added new layers of complexity to the social fabric. Gaelic chiefs, old Celtic laws, and local customs coexisted (sometimes uneasily) with new feudal hierarchies and Norman legal practices.

The Birth of a Distinct Nation

By the end of the 12th century, Scotland had matured into a kingdom recognized by its neighbors and the Pope alike. Its rulers could trace their line back through a rich blend of Pictish, Gaelic, and Norse ancestry, creating a royal identity that symbolized the kingdom's diverse roots.

Yet, the unity was fragile. Old clan rivalries simmered beneath the surface, regional differences persisted, and external threats loomed large. But despite these challenges, the Scots had forged a sense of collective destiny

— a belief in their right to self-determination and their distinctiveness as a people.

This new national identity, tested in coming centuries by war and political upheaval, would become one of Scotland's most enduring legacies. The struggles ahead — for independence, for faith, for survival — would only strengthen it.

As we look back on this period, it is striking how the Scottish story was never one of isolation. It was always a story of meeting and melding: Gaels and Picts becoming Alba; Norman lords building upon Gaelic foundations; monasteries serving as both religious sanctuaries and political think tanks. Each layer, each encounter, added to the richness of what it meant — and still means — to be Scottish.

So, as the sun dips behind a Highland ridge and the first stars prick the evening sky, imagine the ghostly procession of early kings and queens, clan chiefs and monks, all walking through the mists of history, carrying torches that would light the way for generations to come.

Chapter 4: The Wars for Freedom: Wallace, Bruce, and the Fight for Independence

The story of Scotland's independence is one of the most stirring epics in European history — a saga filled with fierce battles, legendary heroes, betrayals, and unyielding spirit. If earlier centuries had laid the foundation for a shared Scottish identity, it was in the crucible of war against England that this identity was truly forged, tested, and immortalized.

The tale begins in the late 13th century, a time when Scotland's relative stability was abruptly shattered by a dynastic crisis. King Alexander III died in 1286 after a tragic riding accident, leaving his only heir, his granddaughter Margaret, known as the Maid of Norway. Her untimely death at sea in 1290 plunged the kingdom into turmoil. Thirteen claimants vied for the crown, most notably John Balliol and Robert Bruce (grandfather to the future king).

Fearing civil war, the Scottish nobles invited England's King Edward I to arbitrate. Edward accepted — but with a cunning twist: he demanded recognition as Scotland's overlord. Under pressure, the Scottish nobles conceded, and John Balliol was crowned king in 1292. Yet from the start, Balliol was a puppet, humiliated by Edward's heavy-handed interference. The proud Scottish nobles seethed under this subjugation, their sense of independence trampled.

The Spark of Rebellion

The tipping point came in 1295 when Balliol, pushed to defiance, formed an alliance with France — the famous "Auld Alliance." Edward responded brutally, invading Scotland in 1296, sacking Berwick, and forcing Balliol to abdicate. The English king even stole the Stone of Destiny from Scone Abbey, a powerful symbol of Scottish sovereignty, and carried it to Westminster Abbey.

It was during this grim period that a new figure emerged from the mists of history — William Wallace. A knight of minor standing, Wallace became a beacon of resistance. In 1297, alongside Andrew Moray, he led a ragtag force of commoners and lesser nobles to a stunning victory at the Battle of Stirling Bridge. Using the terrain to their advantage, the Scots outmaneuvered the heavily armored English, proving that courage and cunning could defeat might.

Wallace was declared Guardian of Scotland, ruling in the name of the imprisoned Balliol. But the fight was far from over. In 1298, Edward returned with a massive army and crushed Wallace at the Battle of Falkirk. Though defeated, Wallace's legend only grew. He embodied the ideal of a free Scotland, willing to fight and die rather than kneel. Eventually captured in 1305, Wallace was taken to London, brutally executed for treason, and his limbs were sent to different parts of Scotland as a grim warning.

Yet his spirit did not die. Instead, it sparked the next, even greater chapter of resistance.

The Rise of Robert the Bruce

Into this chaos stepped Robert Bruce, a man whose ambition matched his patriotism. On February 10, 1306, Bruce took a fateful step: he murdered his rival, John Comyn, in a church at Dumfries — an act that horrified many but cleared his path to the throne. Only weeks later, he was crowned King of Scots at Scone, a bold and dangerous declaration of defiance.

Bruce's early campaigns were disastrous. He was driven into hiding, excommunicated by the church, and saw many of his family members imprisoned or executed. But he did not give up. Like a king in exile from an old ballad, he bided his time, gathered loyal supporters, and launched a guerrilla war from the Highlands.

Slowly, Bruce's fortunes turned. Key victories at Loudoun Hill and the Pass of Brander allowed him to reclaim castles and inspire a weary nation. His charisma and determination gradually won over both nobles and commoners.

The defining moment came in June 1314 at the Battle of Bannockburn, near Stirling. Against overwhelming odds, Bruce's forces — fewer in number and less equipped — decisively defeated Edward II's army. According to tradition, on the eve of battle, Bruce fought and killed an English knight in single combat, boosting his army's morale. The Scottish schiltrons — tight formations of spearmen — proved devastatingly effective against English cavalry charges.

Bannockburn became more than a military victory; it was a national miracle, an affirmation that Scotland could stand free and proud. Following this, Bruce systematically reclaimed Scottish strongholds and forced the English out.

The Declaration of Arbroath: A Nation's Soul

Even after Bannockburn, England refused to recognize Scottish independence. But in 1320, Scotland made a dramatic appeal to the Pope in a document known as the Declaration of Arbroath.

This declaration, signed by Scottish nobles, asserted that Scotland had always been an independent kingdom and that their king ruled by the will of the people, not by divine right or foreign claim. It famously declared:

"For as long as but a hundred of us remain alive, never will we on any conditions be brought under English rule. It is in truth not for glory, nor riches, nor honours that we are fighting, but for freedom — for that alone, which no honest man gives up but with life itself."

This was revolutionary — a medieval articulation of what we now call self-determination. It laid the philosophical foundation for later ideas of popular sovereignty and inspired movements far beyond Scotland's borders.

Finally, in 1328, the Treaty of Edinburgh-Northampton recognized Scotland's independence and Robert the Bruce as king. It was a hard-won triumph after decades of sacrifice.

The Second War of Independence

Sadly, Bruce enjoyed only a few years of peace before his death in 1329. His son, David II, inherited the throne at age five, opening the door to renewed conflict. Edward Balliol, son of the deposed John Balliol, backed by England and disinherited Scottish nobles, invaded in 1332.

Scotland endured yet another grueling series of battles, with Balliol briefly taking the crown before being expelled. David II was forced into exile in France but returned to rule in 1341. In 1346, he was captured by the English at the Battle of Neville's Cross and held prisoner for eleven years.

Despite these setbacks, the Scots never surrendered their independence. In 1357, David II was ransomed and returned, and by the time of his death in 1371, the Stewart dynasty was poised to continue Scotland's royal line.

Legacy of the Wars of Independence

The Wars of Independence did more than preserve Scotland's political sovereignty; they cemented a collective identity rooted in the values of freedom, resilience, and community. Figures like Wallace and Bruce became immortalized not just in chronicles but in songs, poems, and eventually, films.

The saltire flag — the white cross on a blue field — began to emerge as a powerful national symbol during this time, embodying the spirit of defiance and unity. Place names, battle sites, and ancient castles across Scotland still echo these stories. Visitors today can stand at Bannockburn and feel the ground that once trembled with the charge of spearmen; they can wander the ruins of Stirling Castle, where Bruce and his allies plotted, or gaze upon the mighty Wallace Monument.

Perhaps more profoundly, the wars inspired an enduring belief that Scotland was a nation forged not merely by kings or treaties but by the will and courage of its people. This spirit would resonate through future centuries, from the Jacobite risings to the modern independence movement.

The People's Story

Amid the heroics of knights and kings, we must not forget the common people — farmers, fishermen, weavers, and shepherds — who bore the brunt of war. Villages were burned, families scattered, and livelihoods destroyed, yet they held fast to their land and traditions. They provided food and shelter to rebels, carried secret messages, and kept the flame of freedom alive during the darkest nights.

Their quiet bravery reminds us that nations are not built only by grand speeches or dramatic battles but also by the everyday acts of endurance and solidarity that define a people.

As the 14th century drew to a close, Scotland stood battered yet unbowed. It had survived the ambitions of powerful empires, the schemes of rival dynasties, and the storms of internal division. But most importantly, it had emerged with a renewed sense of itself — a small, proud kingdom standing steadfast on the edge of the world, a beacon of defiance and dignity.

Chapter 5: Clans and Castles: The Heartbeat of Highland Life

When we think of Scotland, certain images spring instantly to mind: mist drifting around ancient stone towers, tartan kilts whipping in the Highland wind, bagpipes echoing over green glens. At the heart of these images lies the clan — a social structure that has come to symbolize Scotland's unique spirit of loyalty, kinship, and fierce independence.

The story of the clans is not merely a tale of warriors and tartans; it is a deeply woven tapestry of family, land, politics, and identity. From the Middle Ages into the modern era, clans defined much of Scotland's social landscape, particularly in the Highlands.

The Rise of the Clans

The emergence of the clan system in Scotland traces back to the fragmentation of authority following the fall of the ancient Celtic lordships, especially the Lordship of the Isles. As centralized royal power struggled to extend its reach into the mountainous north and west, local chieftains filled the vacuum.

In the Gaelic sense, a "clan" (from the Gaelic *clann*, meaning "children" or "family") was not simply a collection of blood relatives but an extended family bound together by loyalty to a chief. The chief acted as both patriarch and protector, offering security and leadership in return for loyalty and service.

Land was central to clan identity. Unlike English feudalism, where land ownership was largely transactional, the Highland relationship to land was deeply spiritual and communal. The glens, hills, and lochs were not just resources but living members of the clan's story — places where ancestors fought, loved, and died.

Castles and Strongholds

The clan's power radiated outward from its stronghold — the castle or fortified tower house. These structures were both homes and symbols of authority, often situated on high ground or near strategic waterways.

Imagine a Highland castle at dawn: thick walls of grey stone, banners bearing the clan crest fluttering in the cold air, the faint smell of wood smoke rising from the great hall. Inside, warriors sharpened swords by the hearth, while bards recited tales of ancient battles to wide-eyed children. These strongholds were the beating heart of clan society, where strategy was plotted, justice was administered, and bonds of kinship were strengthened through feasts and celebrations.

Many of Scotland's most iconic castles, such as Eilean Donan, Dunvegan, and Urquhart, began as clan fortresses. Their rugged beauty today still stirs something ancient in the blood, reminding us of a time when life was intimately tied to the rhythms of land and kin.

Tartan and Identity

Each clan developed its own tartan pattern, a distinctive arrangement of colored stripes and checks woven into wool. While tartans likely began as regional patterns rather than strictly clan-specific designs, over time they became closely associated with individual clans, serving as powerful emblems of identity.

Wearing your clan tartan was like wearing your heart on your sleeve. It declared your loyalties, your family, your place in the long chain of ancestors. In times of peace, tartan adorned gatherings and festivals; in times of war, it united warriors on the battlefield.

Beyond its symbolism, tartan offered practical benefits: its thick woolen weave protected against Highland winds and rain, and the earthy colors provided camouflage in the heather and bracken.

The Bardic Tradition and Oral Memory

Within each clan, the bard held a special place of honor. More than a mere entertainer, the bard was the memory-keeper, the voice of the clan's soul. Bards memorized genealogies, recorded battles and alliances, and recited heroic poems that reminded each generation of their heritage and obligations.

Gatherings around the hearth would come alive as the bard began to chant, his words weaving visions of ancient kings, doomed love affairs, and spectral warnings from the otherworld. In this way, stories acted as both entertainment and moral instruction, binding the community together in a shared narrative.

Feuds and Alliances

Clan life was far from idyllic. Competition over grazing lands, fishing rights, or simple insults could ignite bloody feuds lasting generations. Skirmishes often erupted without warning, and revenge killings became part of the grim cycle of Highland life.

Yet alongside these feuds were complex networks of alliances. Marriages between clans were carefully arranged to strengthen ties and secure borders. A marriage contract might include not only dowries but also promises of military aid and non-aggression pacts. In this intricate dance of loyalty and rivalry, the Highlands functioned almost like a living chessboard.

One of the most infamous episodes in clan history is the Massacre of Glencoe in 1692. In this tragedy, members of Clan Campbell, acting under government orders, murdered their hosts from Clan MacDonald after accepting their hospitality — a betrayal so profound it still echoes painfully today in Highland memory.

The Highland Clearances: A Tragic Turning Point

The power and cohesion of the clans began to unravel in the 18th and 19th centuries. Following the failed Jacobite risings — rebellions aimed at restoring the Stuart monarchy — the British government sought to pacify the Highlands and weaken clan structures.

Acts were passed that banned the wearing of tartan, carrying of weapons, and playing of bagpipes (considered instruments of war). Chiefs were incentivized to convert their communal lands into profitable sheep farms, leading to the infamous Highland Clearances.

Entire communities were evicted, homes burned, and families forced to emigrate to urban centers or across the ocean to North America, Australia, and New Zealand. For many, the glens that had sustained their families for centuries became silent and empty.

This period of enforced displacement was not just an economic policy but a cultural assault — an attempt to erase a way of life built on shared land, kinship, and oral tradition. Even today, abandoned crofts and overgrown ruins stand as melancholy witnesses to this lost world.

Resilience and Revival

Despite this devastation, the spirit of the clans did not vanish. The 19th century saw a romantic revival of Highland culture, partly driven by writers like Sir Walter Scott, whose novels and poems celebrated clan heroism and Highland mystique.

Queen Victoria's deep affection for Scotland and her establishment of Balmoral Castle also played a role, popularizing tartan, Highland dress, and pageantry among the British aristocracy and wider public. What had been suppressed as a symbol of rebellion was reimagined as a symbol of Scottish pride.

Today, Highland games, clan gatherings, and tartan festivals are celebrated worldwide. Scots at home and abroad trace their ancestry with pride, wear kilts at weddings, and gather to hear the skirl of the pipes — each act a quiet defiance against the forces that once tried to dismantle their way of life.

The Heartbeat of Scotland

The story of the clans is ultimately the story of belonging: to a family, to a landscape, to a shared memory. The bonds of loyalty and community that defined clan life remain at the core of Scottish identity today.

Whether a person descends from MacDonald, Campbell, Fraser, MacLeod, or any other great clan, they carry within them echoes of ancient glens and starlit gatherings by the fire. They inherit not only names and tartans but a fierce commitment to resilience and honor.

As we wander among the ruins of old strongholds, listen to the pipes over heather hills, or trace the delicate threads of a tartan sash, we feel that pulse — the heartbeat of a people who, though scattered by history, remain united by memory and spirit.

In the end, the story of Scotland's clans and castles is not only a story of the past; it is a living narrative that continues to inspire new generations, inviting all who hear it to take their place in its unfolding saga.

Chapter 6: The Reformation and the Rise of the Kirk

As we cross the threshold into the 16th century, Scotland stands at a spiritual and cultural crossroads. The castles and clans of the Highlands still hum with ancient rhythms, but a powerful wind of change is sweeping through Europe — the Reformation. Scotland, long a deeply Catholic nation intertwined with medieval tradition and papal authority, would soon become a hotbed of religious upheaval, giving rise to a new spiritual identity that would shape its society for centuries: the Presbyterian Kirk.

Seeds of Change

The early tremors of change began quietly in the 1520s and 1530s. Across Europe, reformers like Martin Luther and John Calvin were challenging the Roman Catholic Church, arguing for a return to scriptural authority and simpler worship. In Scotland, whispers of these ideas began to slip in through books, smuggled pamphlets, and returning scholars.

In 1528, the young scholar Patrick Hamilton was burned at the stake in St Andrews for heresy, becoming Scotland's first Protestant martyr. His death sparked curiosity rather than fear. People began to question the lavish lifestyles of bishops and the heavy taxation of church lands. Many saw the old church as corrupt, out of touch with the poor, and deeply entwined with foreign influence from Rome and France.

By the mid-16th century, these murmurs of discontent had swelled into an unstoppable wave.

Enter John Knox

Among the many reformers, none loomed larger than John Knox. Born around 1514, Knox trained as a Catholic priest but soon found himself drawn to the radical ideas of reform. Inspired by Calvin's Geneva, Knox believed in the absolute authority of the Bible and the right of the congregation to resist ungodly rulers — an incendiary idea in a time when monarchs claimed divine right.

Knox returned to Scotland in 1559 like a storm unleashed. His preaching was fiery and uncompromising, calling the Catholic Mass "idolatry" and urging his followers to cleanse the land of spiritual corruption. His sermons inspired riots and the destruction of church images and altars, symbolizing a break not just from Rome but from centuries of inherited belief and ritual.

Knox's influence coalesced around a group known as the "Lords of the Congregation," a coalition of Protestant nobles who shared his vision of a reformed Kirk (church) free from papal control and rooted in local governance.

Mary, Queen of Scots: A Tragic Clash

In this turbulent period rose the figure of Mary, Queen of Scots — young, charismatic, and Catholic to her core. Returning from France in 1561 to claim her throne, Mary embodied the old alliances and traditions that reformers were determined to overthrow.

Her reign was marked by scandal and intrigue: her disastrous marriages, the murder of her second husband Lord Darnley, and her controversial union with James Hepburn, Earl of Bothwell. Her clashes with Knox were legendary; he openly challenged her authority in sermons and private confrontations, accusing her of leading Scotland back into spiritual darkness.

Ultimately, Mary was forced to abdicate in 1567 in favor of her infant son, James VI. She fled to England, only to be imprisoned and eventually executed by her cousin, Elizabeth I. Her fall marked a decisive victory for the Protestant cause in Scotland.

The Birth of the Presbyterian Kirk

With Mary gone and Protestant nobles in power, Scotland formally embraced the Reformation. In 1560, the Scottish Parliament abolished papal authority, banned the Mass, and adopted a new confession of faith heavily influenced by Calvinism.

The newly established Church of Scotland — known simply as the Kirk — took on a distinctive Presbyterian structure. Unlike the hierarchical Catholic Church or the episcopal system in England, the Kirk was governed by assemblies of elders, reflecting a belief in collective decision-making and local autonomy. Ministers were chosen by congregations, emphasizing the community's role in spiritual life.

Knox and his fellow reformers drafted the *First Book of Discipline*, envisioning a society rooted in godly discipline and education. Although financial realities hindered some of their grander plans (such as a nationwide system of parish schools), the emphasis on literacy took deep root. The conviction that every person should read the Bible for themselves led to remarkably high literacy rates, laying the groundwork for Scotland's later intellectual flourishing.

A New Social Ethos

The Kirk's influence extended far beyond Sunday sermons. It shaped everyday life, instilling a strict moral code. The Sabbath was strictly observed, with work and play coming to a standstill. Drinking, dancing, and revelry were frowned upon, and even minor infractions were met with public penance and admonishment from the kirk session — the local governing body.

This rigorous discipline fostered a sense of collective responsibility and self-policing. While to modern eyes it may seem oppressive, to many Scots it instilled a powerful ethic of hard work, thrift, and moral rectitude.

Education became a key priority. As parish schools multiplied, generations of Scots grew up reading not only religious texts but also developing a taste for inquiry and debate. This intellectual foundation would later blossom into the Scottish Enlightenment, when Scotland would punch far above its weight on the global stage in philosophy, science, and economics.

The Struggle with the Crown

Despite its triumph, the Kirk's journey was far from smooth. The Stuart kings, beginning with James VI, had their own vision for church governance. James, and later his son Charles I, favored a more hierarchical, episcopal model, seeing a strong, crown-controlled church as essential to their authority.

This tension exploded in 1637 when Charles I tried to impose an English-style prayer book on the Scottish church. Outraged, Scots from all walks of life signed the National Covenant in 1638, pledging to defend their religious freedoms. This act sparked the Bishops' Wars, which were part of the wider Wars of the Three Kingdoms — a series of conflicts that included the English Civil War.

Scotland became a battleground for the principle of spiritual independence. The Covenanters, as the signatories were called, viewed themselves as defenders of a sacred trust. Their struggle echoed the earlier Wars of Independence against England, reinforcing the narrative of a people determined to govern themselves — both in politics and in faith.

The Enduring Legacy

The Reformation reshaped Scotland profoundly. It transformed not only religious life but also the cultural DNA of the nation. The fierce commitment to local governance, education, and moral discipline born in this era would ripple through future centuries, influencing everything from politics to literature.

Presbyterianism also played a crucial role in shaping Scotland's global footprint. As Scots emigrated across the world — to North America, Australia, and beyond — they carried with them the Presbyterian model of governance and worship. Many Presbyterian churches abroad trace their roots directly to this turbulent period in Scottish history.

At home, even today, the legacy of the Reformation can be felt in the country's cautious attitude toward centralized power, its strong community life, and its emphasis on fairness and egalitarianism. The

Kirk's story is not merely about theology; it is a story of national character, woven into every thread of Scotland's tartan.

The Echo of the Psalms

If you find yourself wandering through a small village kirk on a quiet Sunday morning, you may still hear the unaccompanied singing of metrical psalms, a practice that dates back to the Reformation. The simple, haunting melodies capture something essential: the Scottish soul — resilient, contemplative, steadfast.

It is in these quiet moments, far from the grand battles and fiery sermons, that the true spirit of the Reformation lives on. A spirit that shaped a nation and, in many ways, continues to shape the world.

Chapter 7: Crowns United: A Tale of Two Kingdoms

When the last embers of the Reformation's fires were still smoldering, Scotland faced yet another transformation — this time not of faith but of crowns. In 1603, a single event would reshape the destiny of two nations forever: the Union of the Crowns.

This chapter of Scotland's story is not about sword clashes on misty battlefields but about royal ambition, political maneuvering, and the difficult dance between independence and unity. It is a tale full of intrigue and consequence, revealing both the possibilities and perils of union.

The Accidental King

In 1603, Queen Elizabeth I of England died childless, ending the Tudor dynasty. Her cousin, James VI of Scotland, was next in line, thanks to his great-grandmother Margaret Tudor's marriage to James IV of Scotland. Thus, James, already King of Scots since infancy, ascended the English throne as James I.

For James, this was the culmination of a lifelong dream. He envisioned himself not just as king of two realms but as the ruler of a single, united kingdom: "Great Britain." To him, it symbolized divine providence and practical wisdom. To many Scots and English alike, however, the reality was far more complicated.

James promptly left Edinburgh for London, arriving to cheers and great hopes. But in Scotland, his departure was felt as a profound loss. He would visit only once again, in 1617, leaving day-to-day governance to a privy council in Edinburgh. Though the crowns were now united, the kingdoms remained legally distinct — each with its own parliament, church, and legal system.

Two Kingdoms, Two Churches

While the two crowns shared a monarch, they did not share a faith. England had settled into a moderate Anglicanism under Elizabeth I, retaining bishops and certain rituals. Scotland, however, had fiercely embraced a Presbyterian Kirk, governed by assemblies and free from royal control.

James sought to bring uniformity, promoting bishops in Scotland and pressing for religious conformity. He viewed the Presbyterian system as a threat to royal authority, suspecting that a people who claimed spiritual independence might also claim political independence.

Tensions simmered beneath the surface. The Scots were proud of their Kirk, which they saw as a hard-won treasure, a safeguard of their spiritual and national integrity. Efforts to impose English-style governance only deepened mistrust and resentment.

Seeds of Conflict: Charles I and the Covenant

If James's attempts at religious conformity caused discomfort, his son Charles I's efforts ignited outright revolt. In 1637, Charles introduced a new prayer book modeled on the English liturgy, hoping to align the Scottish Kirk more closely with Anglican practices.

The reaction was swift and furious. Churchgoers hurled stools at ministers who dared to read from the new book — most famously in St Giles' Cathedral in Edinburgh, where a woman named Jenny Geddes is said to have started the riot by shouting, "Dost thou say Mass at my lug?" (Are you saying the Mass in my ear?)

Within months, Scotland erupted in protest. The National Covenant of 1638, a pledge to defend the Kirk and resist religious "innovations," was signed by thousands across the land — nobles, ministers, and common folk alike. This powerful document reaffirmed Scotland's insistence on spiritual and, by extension, national self-determination.

The signing of the Covenant marked the beginning of the Bishops' Wars, which spilled over into the broader Wars of the Three Kingdoms (including the English Civil War). The Scottish Covenanters even marched into England, forming alliances and forcing Charles to negotiate under duress.

Ultimately, Charles was executed in 1649, an event shocking to monarchists throughout Europe. Scotland, however, declared his son Charles II as king, standing alone against the English republic led by Oliver Cromwell.

Cromwell's Conquest and Forced Union

Cromwell, a seasoned military leader and fervent Puritan, responded quickly. He invaded Scotland in 1650, crushing resistance at battles such as Dunbar and Worcester. Under Cromwell's rule, Scotland was incorporated into a "Commonwealth" with England and Ireland — an enforced union rather than a negotiated agreement.

During this time, Scotland lost its independent parliament, and representation at Westminster was minimal and largely symbolic. The Scottish Kirk faced restrictions, though it retained significant local control. Economically, the country struggled, with many families enduring hardship under heavy taxation and military occupation.

After Cromwell's death in 1658, the monarchy was restored in 1660. Charles II returned to power, and Scotland regained a degree of autonomy. Yet, the scars of the forced union and military subjugation left deep wounds, fueling future tensions and anxieties.

The Glorious Revolution and Protestant Succession

As the 17th century neared its end, yet another upheaval reshaped the royal landscape. In 1688, the Glorious Revolution forced the Catholic King James VII of Scotland and II of England to flee in favor of his Protestant daughter Mary and her husband William of Orange.

For many Scots, particularly those committed to Presbyterianism, this shift was welcome. It confirmed Protestant succession and safeguarded the Kirk against a feared Catholic resurgence. Yet, the Highlands, home to many Jacobites (supporters of James and his descendants), remained a powder keg of loyalty to the old Stuart line.

The tension between Jacobites and the ruling Protestant government would soon lead to a series of dramatic uprisings, culminating in the fateful battle on the bleak moor of Culloden — but that is a story for another chapter.

The Path to Political Union

While the crowns had been united since 1603, Scotland and England continued to maintain separate parliaments and laws. However, economic strain and geopolitical anxiety pushed both kingdoms toward closer union.

For Scotland, the late 17th century was marked by economic hardship. The disastrous Darien Scheme, an ill-fated attempt to establish a Scottish colony in Panama, drained national resources and plunged the country into near-bankruptcy.

For England, there was fear that Scotland might choose a different monarch upon Queen Anne's death, potentially inviting French or Jacobite influence. By the early 1700s, both sides saw political union as a strategic necessity.

In 1707, the Acts of Union were passed, formally merging the Scottish and English parliaments into a single British Parliament at Westminster. The Union promised economic access to English colonies and trade networks but also dissolved Scotland's independent legislature — a heavy price that sparked protests across the land.

The Scottish Parliament closed its doors with the now-famous lament: "There's ane end of ane auld sang" — there's an end to an old song. But as history would show, the melody of Scottish nationhood would continue to play, softer but still resolute, waiting for the next crescendo.

Legacy of the Union of the Crowns

The Union of the Crowns in 1603 set in motion a slow, complex dance between integration and autonomy. It offered opportunities for shared strength but also forced Scotland into difficult compromises on identity and governance.

In some ways, this duality — a shared monarchy yet distinct identity — mirrors the tension at the heart of Scotland's soul: a land that cherishes community and kinship yet fiercely guards its independence.

The crowns may have united, and the parliaments may have merged, but the Scottish spirit, forged in the fires of faith and freedom, refused to be subdued. It would find new ways to express itself in culture, literature, and — in time — renewed political movements.

Today, the legacy of the Union lives on in debates about independence and devolution. It remains a chapter that Scots continue to read, re-read, and reinterpret, each generation adding new footnotes to an ever-evolving story.

Chapter 8: Enlightenment and the Age of Ideas

After the turbulence of religious conflicts and dynastic intrigues, Scotland entered an extraordinary new era — a period marked not by swords or sermons, but by ideas. The 18th century ushered in the Scottish Enlightenment, a time when Scotland, small though it was, became a beacon of intellectual brilliance that would illuminate the entire world.

Imagine a candle flickering in a darkened room. Now imagine dozens of candles lighting one after another until the room glows with warmth and clarity. This is what happened to Scotland during the Enlightenment: a sudden, dazzling burst of intellectual light that transformed not only the nation but also humanity's understanding of itself.

The Roots of Brilliance

How did a country once divided by clan feuds and religious wars become a crucible for reason and progress? The seeds had been sown by earlier reforms — the Reformation's emphasis on literacy and individual interpretation of scripture meant that ordinary Scots were encouraged to read and think critically.

By the early 18th century, Scotland boasted some of the highest literacy rates in Europe. Parish schools dotted the landscape, and universities in Edinburgh, Glasgow, Aberdeen, and St Andrews flourished as centers of learning. The Kirk's insistence on education for moral and spiritual reasons had, ironically, laid the groundwork for a revolution in secular thought.

At the same time, the Acts of Union in 1707, though controversial, opened access to new economic markets and cultural exchanges. Scottish merchants and scholars traveled more widely, bringing back new ideas and challenges to old ways of thinking.

The Edinburgh of the Mind

Edinburgh, often called the "Athens of the North," became the heart of this intellectual ferment. By day, it was a bustling city of trade and law; by night, its smoky taverns and drawing rooms hummed with debate.

Philosophers, scientists, poets, and economists gathered to discuss everything from human nature to natural sciences, from political economy to moral philosophy. These conversations weren't confined to elite salons — they spilled into coffeehouses and onto cobbled streets, where students and artisans alike might join the fray.

Titans of Thought

Among the constellation of Enlightenment thinkers, several Scottish stars shone brightest.

David Hume, with his warm wit and radical skepticism, challenged traditional notions of religion and causality. His *Treatise of Human Nature* proposed that human behavior was driven more by emotion than by reason alone, a controversial idea that laid the foundations for modern psychology.

Adam Smith, another towering figure, revolutionized economics with *The Wealth of Nations*. Published in 1776, this book argued for free markets and the "invisible hand" of self-interest guiding economic prosperity. Smith's insights continue to shape global economic policies centuries later.

James Hutton, often called the "father of modern geology," proposed the idea of deep time — that Earth was shaped over unimaginable eons rather than in a few thousand years as traditionally believed. This concept reshaped our understanding of the planet and laid the groundwork for Charles Darwin's later work.

Francis Hutcheson, a moral philosopher, argued that humans possessed an innate "moral sense," a revolutionary idea that emphasized empathy and social harmony over cold legalism.

Thomas Reid, founder of the Scottish Common Sense school of philosophy, pushed back against Hume's skepticism, arguing that certain truths were self-evident and fundamental to human experience.

These were not isolated geniuses but members of a vibrant, interconnected community that believed knowledge should serve humanity, improve society, and uplift the spirit.

Science and Innovation

The Enlightenment spirit wasn't confined to philosophy and economics. Advances in medicine, engineering, and chemistry flowed from Scottish minds.

William Cullen, a physician and chemist, introduced the concept of "nervous energy" and inspired Joseph Black, who discovered carbon dioxide and laid the foundations for modern thermochemistry.

James Watt, though working from ideas developed in England, was a Scottish innovator who transformed the steam engine. His improvements powered factories, ships, and locomotives, helping to spark the Industrial Revolution.

James Boswell, while better known as a biographer, chronicled this era with an unmatched literary flair. His *Life of Samuel Johnson* remains one of the great biographies in English literature and captures the intellectual vivacity of the period.

The Social Dimension

The Enlightenment was not merely academic; it was social and deeply practical. Civic improvement societies sprang up across cities and towns, working to clean streets, build hospitals, and establish libraries.

Reading societies, debating clubs, and lending libraries became common even in smaller towns. The ideal of the "improving Scotsman" — self-educated, industrious, and civic-minded — took hold as a cultural aspiration.

Scottish Enlightenment thinkers believed in *progress*: the conviction that society could and should be improved by reason, education, and moral betterment. This idea profoundly shaped modern liberal democracies and reform movements across the Atlantic.

The Global Ripple

Scotland's Enlightenment ideas did not stay within its misty glens. They crossed oceans and shaped the emerging American republic. Many signatories of the Declaration of Independence were influenced by Scottish philosophers, and several early American universities drew inspiration from Scotland's emphasis on practical, moral, and scientific education.

Scottish emigrants carried Enlightenment values around the world — to Canada, Australia, and beyond — embedding concepts of fairness, education, and self-reliance into new societies.

A Literary Renaissance

While philosophers debated moral sense and economists sketched markets, poets and novelists were no less busy.

Robert Burns, the "ploughman poet," celebrated the dignity of common folk in his verses, bridging Enlightenment ideals with folk tradition. His lines — "A man's a man for a' that" — echoed the Enlightenment faith in universal human worth.

Sir Walter Scott, with his historical novels like *Waverley*, helped cement Scotland's romantic image while also exploring deep questions about tradition, loyalty, and change. His works captivated readers across Europe and America and gave Scotland a mythic status that endures today.

The Shadow Side

Yet, the Scottish Enlightenment was not without contradictions. Many thinkers supported or benefited from the British Empire and its colonial ventures, including the transatlantic slave trade. Their lofty ideals of liberty and equality often did not extend to enslaved peoples or colonized nations, a moral blind spot that modern scholars continue to examine and critique.

This tension between ideals and practice serves as a reminder that even the brightest intellectual periods are shaped by their historical contexts — both the enlightenment they bring and the shadows they cast.

A Legacy Still Alive

The Scottish Enlightenment left a legacy that continues to pulse through the veins of Scotland and the world. Its ideals echo in the country's education system, its emphasis on fairness and debate, and its persistent questioning spirit.

Visit Edinburgh today and you'll find statues of Hume and Smith, university halls named for Reid and Hutcheson, and libraries preserving centuries of inquiry. Attend a public lecture or wander into a bustling café, and you'll feel the same intellectual electricity that once crackled through smoky taverns centuries ago.

In a world still grappling with questions of truth, progress, and human nature, Scotland's Age of Ideas reminds us that knowledge is not merely to be accumulated, but to be shared — to light candles in the darkness and to uplift the human spirit.

Chapter 9: From Crofts to Coal: The Industrial Transformation

As the glow of the Enlightenment lit minds across Scotland, another fire was beginning to burn — this one in the heart of furnaces, beneath the ground, and along the banks of great rivers. This was the fire of the Industrial Revolution, a force that would reshape the nation's landscape, economy, and way of life in ways even the philosophers of Edinburgh could scarcely have imagined.

The story of Scotland's industrial transformation is a tale of ambition and ingenuity, but also of hardship and loss. It is a chapter written in soot and steel, in the clang of shipyards, and in the quiet resilience of communities uprooted by change.

The Rise of Industrial Scotland

In the late 18th and 19th centuries, Scotland moved swiftly from a predominantly rural, agrarian society to a hub of industry and commerce. Small crofts and scattered farms gave way to vast textile mills, roaring shipyards, and coal mines that burrowed deep into the earth.

Glasgow, once a modest medieval town, transformed into the "Second City of the Empire." Its shipyards along the River Clyde built vessels that carried goods — and empire — to every corner of the globe. The city's skyline, once dominated by church spires, now bristled with factory chimneys spewing black smoke into the gray Scottish sky.

Meanwhile, Edinburgh became a center of finance and intellectual capital, its elegant Georgian streets a sharp contrast to the industrial grime of the west. Dundee rose as a powerhouse of jute production, its mills echoing with the sounds of looms and bustling workers.

Coal, Iron, and Steam

Coal was the beating heart of this transformation. Vast coal seams in the Lowlands fueled everything from home hearths to steam engines. Miners toiled underground in dark, dangerous conditions, their lives dictated by the rhythm of shifts and the whims of the mine owners.

Above ground, ironworks turned molten ore into rails, bridges, and machinery. The great iron foundries of Lanarkshire and Ayrshire fed the expansion of the railway network, which in turn accelerated industrial growth by connecting even the most remote towns to markets across Britain.

James Watt's improvements to the steam engine revolutionized not only factories but also transportation. Steam locomotives shrieked across the countryside, linking cities and shortening journeys that once took days into mere hours. Steamships from the Clyde carried emigrants, coal, and manufactured goods far beyond Scotland's misty shores.

Textile Titans and Mill Towns

Textiles were another cornerstone of Scotland's industrial surge. In towns like Paisley, mills churned out wool and cotton goods destined for British and colonial markets. Paisley's signature shawls became fashion statements across Europe and America, their intricate patterns drawing from ancient Celtic and Eastern designs.

In the northeast, linen and jute dominated. Dundee, known as "Juteopolis," processed raw jute from India into sacks, ropes, and sailcloth. The industry offered employment to thousands — especially women and children — but at the cost of long hours, low wages, and hazardous working conditions.

The mills demanded labor, and entire families left the countryside for crowded urban tenements. Children worked from a young age, their small fingers nimble enough for dangerous machinery. Women carried heavy loads in lint-filled air, coughing as they returned each evening to crowded, damp lodgings.

Urban Life: Promise and Peril

Cities swelled with migrants from rural Scotland and Ireland. Glasgow, Edinburgh, Dundee, and Aberdeen grew rapidly, their populations surging far beyond what aging infrastructure could handle.

Tenements rose quickly to house workers. These multi-story buildings were often dark, damp, and overcrowded, with entire families crammed into a single room. Sanitation was poor, disease spread easily, and infant mortality rates soared. Yet, amid these hardships, a vibrant community life emerged. Neighbors looked after each other, shared meager resources, and found solace in communal gatherings, music, and the bonds of shared struggle.

Public health crises eventually forced reforms. Clean water systems, public baths, and social housing initiatives were introduced, often driven by philanthropists and reform-minded politicians inspired by Enlightenment ideals.

Social Upheaval and Labor Movements

The harsh realities of industrial labor bred resentment and resistance. In the early 19th century, workers began to organize, demanding shorter hours, safer conditions, and fair wages.

Weavers in the Clyde Valley, known as the Radical Weavers, became early leaders in the fight for workers' rights. Their strikes and protests were met with fierce suppression from landowners and factory bosses, but they planted the seeds of Scotland's strong trade union tradition.

Later, miners and dockworkers followed, forming unions that became vital voices for Scotland's working class. Their struggles laid the foundation for modern labor laws and the broader social democratic movements that would shape Scottish politics in the 20th century.

New Lanark: A Visionary Experiment

Amid the grimness, some bright spots emerged. The mill town of New Lanark, under the management of Robert Owen from 1800, became a pioneering example of humane industrialism.

Owen believed that workers thrived with fair treatment and education. He reduced working hours, built decent housing, opened a cooperative store, and created a school for children — including one of the first nursery schools in the world.

New Lanark attracted visitors from across Europe, inspiring early socialist and cooperative movements. Though Owen's vision did not spread as widely as he hoped, New Lanark stands today as a UNESCO World Heritage site and a testament to the possibility of compassionate capitalism.

The Price of Progress

Scotland's industrial boom brought unprecedented wealth, but it was unevenly distributed. The owners of mines, mills, and shipyards amassed fortunes and built grand townhouses, while many workers lived lives of hardship and insecurity.

The landscape, too, bore scars. Rivers turned black with chemical runoff, and the air in industrial towns thickened with soot. Crofts and highland glens emptied as people left ancestral lands, a quiet echo of the Highland Clearances now driven by economic rather than military force.

Yet, these same industrial advancements also laid the groundwork for Scotland's global influence. Scottish engineers, doctors, and merchants spread across the British Empire and beyond, bringing with them knowledge, technologies, and — sometimes controversially — the imperial ambitions of the era.

The Decline and the Echoes

After World War I, Scotland's industrial might began to wane. Global competition, technological changes, and economic crises in the 20th century led to the decline of heavy industries. Shipyards closed, mines were abandoned, and once-thriving mill towns faced mass unemployment and social hardship.

However, these communities adapted with remarkable resilience. Many turned to new industries such as electronics and oil, while others reinvented themselves through tourism and cultural heritage. The discovery of North Sea oil in the 1970s brought a new, if temporary, wave of prosperity and debate about economic independence.

Today, visitors can explore remnants of this industrial past: towering cranes on the Clyde, preserved mills in Dundee, and mining museums in Lanarkshire. Each stands as a silent witness to a time when Scotland helped drive the engines of the modern world.

A Nation Transformed

The industrial era left Scotland forever changed. It transformed a land of crofters and clan chiefs into a modern, urban society, forged a powerful working-class consciousness, and connected Scotland to the wider world in profound new ways.

But perhaps its most lasting legacy is in the spirit it nurtured: a fierce pride in craftsmanship, an unyielding commitment to community, and a belief in the dignity of labor. These qualities, born in the furnaces and shipyards, continue to shape Scotland's story today.

Chapter 10: Tartan, Bagpipes, and Myths: The Cultural Soul of Scotland

If you close your eyes and imagine Scotland, what comes to mind? The sweep of mist across glens, a lone piper silhouetted against a rising sun, a swirl of tartan at a highland dance. These vivid images are not simply clichés; they are expressions of a rich and living cultural soul — a legacy carried forward by centuries of tradition, struggle, and celebration.

While political and economic changes reshaped the land, it was in the realm of culture where the heart of Scotland beat loudest and longest. In this chapter, we explore the traditions and symbols that together form the unique tapestry of Scottish identity.

Tartan: Patterns of Belonging

Tartan is perhaps the most instantly recognizable symbol of Scotland. Its bright checks and stripes, woven into thick woolen cloth, carry stories of kinship, land, and legacy.

Although tartan designs have existed in Scotland since at least the third century, their close association with clan identity crystallized in the 16th and 17th centuries. By the 18th century, each clan had developed distinct tartan patterns, which functioned almost like a family crest, worn proudly to signal loyalty and heritage.

After the failed Jacobite uprisings of the 18th century, the wearing of tartan was banned under the Dress Act of 1746 as part of a campaign to break Highland identity and suppress further rebellion. Yet, rather than destroy tartan, this act elevated it to a symbol of resistance and pride.

When the ban was lifted in 1782, tartan experienced a dramatic resurgence. Romantic revivalists, including Sir Walter Scott, helped reframe tartan as a symbol of noble Highland valor. By the time of King George IV's visit to Edinburgh in 1822 — orchestrated by Scott himself — tartan was firmly established as Scotland's national dress.

Today, tartan is worn around the world at weddings, ceilidhs, and Highland games. Whether displayed on a kilt, a sash, or a scarf, it connects Scots and those of Scottish descent to a centuries-old story of defiance, resilience, and belonging.

The Bagpipes: Scotland's Voice in the Wind

If tartan is Scotland's visual emblem, the bagpipes are its voice. Their haunting, powerful tones evoke feelings of pride, melancholy, and celebration — often all at once.

The bagpipes have ancient roots, possibly brought to Scotland by Norse or Roman influences. By the 15th and 16th centuries, they had become fixtures in Highland life. They accompanied warriors into battle, their piercing call meant to inspire the troops and terrify opponents. The piper was a crucial figure in every clan, carrying not only the pipes but also the emotional spirit of the people.

After the suppression of the clans, bagpipes were also targeted as instruments of rebellion. Yet, like tartan, they survived — reimagined in the 19th century as emblems of Scottish martial pride and romanticism.

Today, from the Royal Edinburgh Military Tattoo to quiet ceremonies at war memorials, bagpipes continue to echo Scotland's deepest emotions. Whether lamenting the fallen or celebrating a wedding, they embody the complexity of the Scottish spirit: fierce yet tender, communal yet deeply personal.

The Highland Games: Strength and Celebration

Every summer, fields across Scotland and the Scottish diaspora transform into arenas of strength, agility, and cultural pride during the Highland Games.

Dating back to at least the 11th century, these games originally served as gatherings to choose the clan's strongest warriors and most skilled performers. Contests like the caber toss, stone put, and hammer throw celebrated not just physical might but also precision and grace.

Beyond athletics, the games were (and still are) deeply social events. Pipe bands march, Highland dancers perform intricate steps, and families gather to reconnect with their heritage. In the diaspora communities — from North America to New Zealand — Highland Games have become vital touchstones, sustaining and sharing Scottish culture across the globe.

Folklore: A World of Myths and Spirits

Scotland's misty landscapes are alive with stories. Every loch, glen, and mountain seems to harbor its own legend, creating a rich tapestry of folklore that still influences the national imagination today.

Perhaps the most famous is the Loch Ness Monster, or "Nessie," whose sightings stretch back to the 6th century. Whether viewed as a remnant dinosaur or a playful hoax, Nessie captures the blend of mystery and magic so central to Scottish storytelling.

Then there are the kelpies — shape-shifting water spirits often taking the form of horses. Beautiful and beguiling, they lure unsuspecting travelers into the depths. The Cailleach, the ancient goddess of winter, is said to shape the mountains with her staff and summon snow with her breath. Selkies, seals that transform into humans, whisper tales of love and loss along stormy coasts.

These myths and creatures are not merely quaint stories; they embody deep connections to nature, respect for the unseen world, and warnings about pride and folly. They remain vibrant in literature, art, and tourism today, inviting visitors to see beyond the physical landscape into a world shimmering with wonder.

Music and Dance: The Pulse of the People

Scottish music and dance are as varied as the land itself. From the lilting tunes of the fiddle to the foot-stomping reels at a ceilidh, music has always been at the heart of social life.

Ceilidhs (pronounced "kay-lees") are traditional gatherings that combine music, dance, and storytelling. Originally held in village halls or even barns, ceilidhs were — and still are — opportunities for community bonding. Young and old alike join hands for lively dances like the Gay Gordons and the Dashing White Sergeant, laughter echoing late into the night.

Ballads and folk songs carry centuries of history, love, and loss. The works of Robert Burns, Scotland's national bard, are often sung at gatherings. His "Auld Lang Syne" has crossed every border, sung to ring in the New Year around the world, reminding us of friendship and shared memories.

Handfasting: Ties that Bind

Among Scotland's oldest traditions is handfasting — the symbolic binding of hands during a marriage ceremony. Originally a form of betrothal or trial marriage, handfasting dates back to pagan times when unions were often made "for a year and a day" before being formalized.

Today, couples worldwide incorporate handfasting into wedding ceremonies, celebrating love in a way that feels deeply connected to the land and ancient rhythms. The simple act of tying hands with tartan or ribbon embodies the enduring themes of unity and shared fate.

A Living Culture

Scottish culture is not frozen in time, nor is it simply an echo of the past. It lives and breathes, evolving with each generation. Young musicians fuse traditional tunes with rock and electronic beats; modern designers reinvent tartan on global runways; artists reinterpret ancient myths for new audiences.

Yet, through all these changes, the essence remains: a love for story, a reverence for land and community, and a spirit that refuses to be tamed.

The Heartbeat Continues

As the evening falls over the Highlands and the last strains of a fiddle fade into the purple dusk, one can feel the presence of countless souls who danced, sang, and dreamed before us. Tartan, bagpipes, myths, and music are not relics; they are Scotland's heartbeat — steady, wild, and profoundly human.

Wherever Scots gather — whether in a glen in Skye or at a Highland Games in Canada — that heartbeat pulses strong, reminding them of who they are and inviting the world to join in the dance.

Chapter 11: Across the Seas: The Scottish Diaspora

Scotland is a land of deep roots — of ancient stones, family lineages, and enduring traditions. Yet, paradoxically, it is also a nation defined by movement. For centuries, Scots have taken to the seas, leaving their rugged glens and bustling cities to seek new lives far beyond their misty homeland.

This great exodus, known as the Scottish diaspora, has left footprints across every continent, shaping communities from Nova Scotia to New Zealand. Their journeys tell a story of hardship and hope, loss and reinvention — and of a spirit too wild to be confined to one small corner of the earth.

Early Waves of Migration

The story of Scots moving abroad begins long before the modern age. Medieval mercenaries known as "gallowglasses" traveled to Ireland to fight for Irish chieftains as early as the 13th century, bringing with them fierce Highland fighting techniques and Gaelic cultural influences.

Later, during the 17th century, economic hardship, religious conflicts, and political instability drove more Scots abroad. Some fled as Covenanters after the brutal religious persecutions of the Restoration era. Others crossed the Atlantic as indentured servants, often under grim conditions.

These early migrations set the pattern for what would become a massive movement of people over the next two centuries.

The Highland Clearances: A Painful Exodus

The Highland Clearances of the 18th and 19th centuries marked one of the most dramatic chapters in Scottish emigration. Landowners, seeking to increase profits, evicted tenant farmers (crofters) to replace them with sheep, which were more lucrative in the booming wool trade.

Families who had worked the same patches of land for generations found their homes burned and their communities dismantled. Some were forced into coastal villages to scrape out a living fishing and kelping (gathering seaweed for fertilizer and industry), but many had no choice but to leave Scotland altogether.

They boarded ships bound for North America, Australia, and New Zealand — voyages filled with uncertainty and sorrow. On these ships, entire clans would huddle together, carrying what few possessions they could manage, along with seeds, tools, and tartans.

Though many were driven by necessity, their descendants would become pioneers, carving new communities out of forests, prairies, and distant shores.

Canada: The New Scotland

Nowhere is the Scottish imprint stronger than in Canada. In Nova Scotia — Latin for "New Scotland" — Gaelic once echoed in the hills as vibrantly as it did in the Highlands.

Cape Breton Island, in particular, became a stronghold of Gaelic culture. Emigrants built stone churches reminiscent of their old parishes, held ceilidhs in barns, and played the fiddle tunes that had once soared over Loch Lomond. Even today, visitors to Cape Breton can hear Gaelic spoken, see tartan proudly displayed, and feel the same warmth of Highland hospitality.

Further west, Scots helped build cities like Winnipeg and Vancouver, bringing with them skills in engineering, trade, and governance. Scots were instrumental in the fur trade, serving as traders and explorers for the Hudson's Bay Company, mapping vast swathes of what would become Canada.

America: From Frontiers to Cities

In the United States, Scots and Scots-Irish (descendants of Lowland Scots who had first settled in Ulster, Ireland) played vital roles from the colonial period onward.

The Scots-Irish settled primarily in the Appalachian region, where their independent spirit and Presbyterian faith flourished. Their music — blending Scottish, Irish, and American influences — became the roots of what we know today as bluegrass and country music.

Scots were also prominent among the founding fathers and early leaders. Signers of the Declaration of Independence included men of Scottish heritage, and the Presbyterian model of governance informed early American political thought.

In cities like New York, Philadelphia, and Boston, Scottish societies and clubs sprang up to support new immigrants, preserve traditions, and provide a sense of belonging in an unfamiliar world.

Australia and New Zealand: Building New Worlds

Across the globe, Scots arrived in Australia and New Zealand during the 19th century, drawn by opportunities for land, gold, and freedom from rigid social hierarchies.

In Australia, they became farmers, miners, and urban leaders. Towns like Melbourne and Adelaide saw significant Scottish influence in education and civic life. The Presbyterian Church established schools and universities, emphasizing literacy and self-improvement — values deeply rooted in Scottish culture.

In New Zealand, Scots settled heavily in Otago and Southland, founding the city of Dunedin (its name derived from Dùn Èideann, the Gaelic name for Edinburgh). Here, they built churches and schools, organized Highland games, and even revived Gaelic choirs.

Africa and Beyond

Scottish missionaries, doctors, and engineers also made their way to Africa and Asia, driven by religious conviction and curiosity. Figures like David Livingstone, the famed explorer and missionary, left indelible marks on maps and minds alike.

Livingstone's writings helped shape Western perceptions of Africa and fueled anti-slavery movements back home. Yet, as with all colonial endeavors, this legacy is complex — a blend of humanitarian zeal and imperial complicity that historians continue to unpack.

Keeping the Flame Alive

Wherever they settled, Scots carried more than just physical belongings; they carried songs, dances, poems, and prayers. Highland games, St. Andrew's societies, Burns suppers, and piping competitions became lifelines to a shared past.

Each January 25th, from New York to Auckland, Scots gather to celebrate Robert Burns with whisky, haggis, and recitations of his poems. At these tables, the old stories live on, and new ones are born.

Dual Identity: Home and Away

For many descendants of emigrant Scots, identity is a patchwork quilt — stitched from fragments of their ancestral homeland and the new cultures they inhabit. They feel the pull of both worlds, balancing the rugged independence of their forebears with the realities of life in Canada, America, or Australia.

In some ways, the Scottish diaspora embodies the best of Scotland's spirit: adaptable yet proud, deeply communal yet fiercely individual. Their contributions — from pioneering industries and shaping national politics to enriching global culture with music and dance — continue to ripple outward.

Coming Full Circle

In recent decades, many descendants have returned to Scotland, tracing roots in churchyards, walking the highland paths of their ancestors, and studying Gaelic anew. These "homecomings" reflect a powerful human desire: to know where we come from and to connect the storylines of the past with those of the present.

Meanwhile, Scotland has embraced its global family, hosting clan gatherings, promoting cultural festivals, and supporting worldwide Scottish societies. The sense of kinship transcends oceans, binding together millions in a shared tapestry.

A Nation Without Borders

Scotland may be small on a map, but through its diaspora, it has become a nation without borders — its heartbeat echoing in Canadian forests, Australian deserts, Appalachian hollows, and African mission stations.

Every fiddle tune in Cape Breton, every ceilidh in Dunedin, every Burns supper in Chicago is a reminder that Scotland lives not only in one rugged northern land but wherever its people carry its spirit.

In the end, the Scottish story is not just about staying rooted but about carrying those roots across the world — and watching them flower in countless new forms.

Chapter 12: Scotland and the Empire: Partners and Paradoxes

The story of Scotland is often told as one of fierce independence — a nation of rebels, poets, and dreamers standing resolutely against outside domination. Yet there is another, more complex chapter to this story: Scotland's deep and sometimes uneasy relationship with the British Empire.

While Scotland resisted English conquest for centuries, after the Act of Union in 1707, it became a key partner in building and managing one of the largest empires in human history. This chapter explores that paradox: how a land so committed to its own identity helped forge a global empire, and how that empire, in turn, shaped Scotland.

The Union and Opportunity

The Act of Union created a single political and economic framework that offered Scots new opportunities. Before 1707, Scots were often barred from trading with English colonies. After the union, the gates swung open.

Ambitious Scots poured into the merchant houses of London and Bristol, joined shipping ventures to the Caribbean, or set sail for the American colonies. Enterprising traders set up tobacco plantations in Virginia and sugar estates in Jamaica, creating a new class of wealthy Scottish merchants known as the "tobacco lords" and "sugar barons."

Glasgow, in particular, thrived, transforming from a modest town on the Clyde to a commercial powerhouse. Elegant mansions lined its streets, funded by profits from slave-grown commodities.

Military Service and Migration

Scotland also became a major recruiting ground for the British army. Highland regiments, once feared as rebels, were now celebrated as elite warriors of the empire.

After the Jacobite rebellions of the 18th century, the British government realized that the martial spirit of the Highlands could be harnessed rather than suppressed. Regiments such as the Black Watch became symbols of Scottish pride and imperial strength, fighting in conflicts from India to North America.

For many young Scots, military service offered escape from poverty and the promise of adventure — even as it often meant enforcing colonial rule over others.

Beyond soldiers, Scots also migrated across the empire as engineers, doctors, missionaries, and administrators. They built railways in India, administered colonies in Africa, and established schools and hospitals from Canada to New Zealand.

The Missionary Zeal

The 19th century saw an explosion of missionary activity, with Scots at the forefront. Inspired by evangelical revivalism and a deeply ingrained Presbyterian duty to "civilize" the world, Scottish missionaries fanned out across Africa, Asia, and the Pacific.

Perhaps the most famous was David Livingstone, who ventured deep into Africa, driven by both exploration and the goal of ending the slave trade. His journeys fascinated the public and made him a national hero, though modern perspectives reveal the complexities and unintended consequences of his work.

Missionaries often brought education and medicine, but they also imposed Western values and undermined local cultures. Their legacies are thus complicated — a mixture of altruism, cultural arrogance, and genuine compassion.

The Dark Shadow of Slavery

A critical part of Scotland's imperial story is its involvement in the transatlantic slave trade. While Scotland itself had no plantations, its economic fortunes were deeply intertwined with slavery.

Many of Glasgow's tobacco lords and sugar merchants depended on slave labor to generate their immense wealth. Scottish merchants invested in slave ships, and Scottish overseers managed plantations in the Caribbean.

Some Scots, such as James McQueen, actively defended slavery as an economic necessity. Yet, in later decades, Scots also joined abolitionist movements, speaking out against the brutalities of the trade they had once profited from.

This moral reckoning is ongoing today. In recent years, universities and institutions across Scotland have begun to confront and acknowledge these historical ties, leading to public debates and memorial projects.

Intellectual and Economic Influence

The Scottish Enlightenment — with its emphasis on reason, improvement, and moral philosophy — provided ideological justification for empire. Many Scots sincerely believed they were spreading "civilization" and progress, despite the violent realities of colonial rule.

Scottish engineers and educators helped shape colonial infrastructure and governance. Railways in India, plantations in the Caribbean, and mines in Africa all bore the marks of Scottish expertise.

Meanwhile, the global empire brought new wealth back to Scotland. Tea, tobacco, sugar, and textiles filled Scottish warehouses, fueling local industries and creating jobs. Cities like Dundee prospered by producing jute bags for empire-wide shipping; Edinburgh and Glasgow thrived as centers of finance and commerce.

Resistance and Complex Identities

Yet, even as Scots helped build and administer the empire, they retained a strong sense of their own identity — sometimes in tension with Britishness.

In the colonies, Scottish settlers often formed their own communities, preserving Gaelic songs, Highland games, and Presbyterian churches.

They saw themselves as both Scottish and British, a duality that could be both empowering and confusing.

In India and Africa, some Scots formed close bonds with local communities, learning languages and advocating for rights. Others enforced harsh colonial policies with unwavering loyalty to the crown.

This mixture of complicity, pride, and moral questioning created a uniquely Scottish imperial legacy: one that resists easy categorization and continues to provoke debate.

The Empire's Decline and Return Home

The 20th century brought decolonization and a rethinking of empire. As colonies gained independence, many Scots returned home, bringing with them new perspectives and sometimes a deep sense of loss for the world they had helped build.

Meanwhile, migration from former colonies began to reshape Scotland itself. New Scots from South Asia, Africa, and the Caribbean added their voices and cultures to Scotland's evolving identity, creating a more diverse and vibrant society.

Reconciling the Past

In the 21st century, Scotland has begun to reckon with its imperial legacy. Statues of imperial figures are reinterpreted or removed, museum exhibits are updated to include stories of colonized peoples, and public discussions address the historical benefits that Scotland reaped from empire — alongside the harms inflicted.

Universities like Glasgow have researched their links to slavery and pledged reparative initiatives, including scholarships for descendants of enslaved people. Artists and writers explore the emotional and ethical complexities of Scotland's imperial past, sparking new national conversations.

A Shared Inheritance

Scotland's role in the British Empire is a story of paradoxes. It is a story of a people who fiercely defended their own independence yet helped subdue the independence of others; who cherished community and kinship yet participated in a global system of exploitation; who produced humanitarian heroes and harsh administrators alike.

This inheritance shapes Scotland today — in its architecture, in its cultural institutions, and in the very questions it asks about itself. It challenges Scots to examine the tension between pride in achievements abroad and sorrow for injustices committed.

Looking Forward

As Scotland looks toward the future — contemplating its own place in Europe and the world — the lessons of the empire loom large. They urge a new generation to ask: What does it mean to belong? What responsibilities do we have to each other across borders? How do we honor the richness of our heritage while acknowledging its shadows?

In these questions, we hear echoes of the same restless, questioning spirit that has defined Scotland for centuries — a spirit always looking beyond the horizon, always wrestling with the complexities of identity, always seeking to reconcile pride with conscience.

Chapter 13: The Spirit of Independence: From Arbroath to Holyrood

Beneath the dramatic skies of Scotland lies a spirit that refuses to be subdued — a yearning for self-determination that echoes across centuries. From the rugged castles of medieval kings to the debating chambers of modern parliaments, the Scottish spirit of independence has been a defining current in the nation's story.

This chapter is a journey through that restless spirit: the declarations, the uprisings, and the democratic debates that have shaped Scotland's quest to govern itself.

The Declaration of Arbroath: A Bold Beginning

The seeds of Scottish independence were famously sown in 1320 with the Declaration of Arbroath. Written to Pope John XXII during the Wars of Independence, this document was more than a plea for diplomatic recognition — it was a fiery assertion of a nation's right to exist.

Its most famous lines still stir hearts today:

"For as long as but a hundred of us remain alive, never will we on any conditions be brought under English rule. It is in truth not for glory, nor riches, nor honours that we are fighting, but for freedom — for that alone, which no honest man gives up but with life itself."

The Declaration marked Scotland as one of the earliest nations to articulate the principle that sovereignty belongs to the people, not the king. It inspired future generations and set the tone for centuries of resistance and self-assertion.

The Union and the Jacobite Risings

Despite this fierce independence, economic hardship and dynastic maneuvering led to the Act of Union in 1707, merging the Scottish and

English parliaments. Many Scots felt betrayed, seeing the Union as a loss of national sovereignty in exchange for economic gain.

This tension fueled the Jacobite risings — a series of rebellions in the 17th and 18th centuries seeking to restore the exiled Stuart line to the throne. The most famous, the 1745 rising led by Charles Edward Stuart (Bonnie Prince Charlie), ended in heartbreak at the Battle of Culloden.

Though ultimately crushed, the Jacobite cause became woven into Scottish cultural memory as a symbol of lost sovereignty and romantic defiance. Highland dress, songs, and legends celebrated this doomed struggle, keeping the ember of independence glowing beneath the surface.

Industrial Scotland and the Union

As Scotland industrialized in the 18th and 19th centuries, economic ties with England deepened. Many Scots saw the Union as a vehicle for progress and prosperity, with Glasgow and Edinburgh becoming centers of commerce and intellect.

Yet the sense of a distinct Scottish identity never faded. Robert Burns's poetry and Sir Walter Scott's novels rekindled national pride, while Highland games and tartan revivals celebrated cultural uniqueness. The tension between economic pragmatism and emotional allegiance to independence continued to shape Scottish life.

The Birth of Home Rule Movements

In the late 19th and early 20th centuries, as democratic reforms spread across the UK, Scottish calls for self-government gained renewed momentum. Inspired by Irish Home Rule campaigns, Scottish activists began pressing for their own parliament to manage domestic affairs.

The Scottish Home Rule Association, formed in 1886, pushed for devolution rather than full independence. These early movements emphasized control over education, health, and local governance rather than outright separation.

Yet despite widespread support, political inertia and the focus on empire delayed meaningful progress. Scotland remained firmly under Westminster's control well into the 20th century.

Post-War Awakening and the SNP

After World War II, social and economic shifts reignited the independence debate. Deindustrialization hit Scotland hard, fueling resentment against perceived neglect by London.

The Scottish National Party (SNP), founded in 1934, began to gain traction. Initially a fringe movement, the SNP steadily grew, positioning itself as the champion of full independence rather than limited devolution.

A pivotal moment came in 1979, when a referendum was held on establishing a Scottish Assembly. Though a majority voted "Yes," turnout failed to meet a required threshold, and the initiative collapsed, deepening frustration and fueling a sense of disenfranchisement.

Devolution and the Creation of the Scottish Parliament

The tide turned decisively in the 1990s. A second referendum in 1997 resulted in a resounding "Yes" for a devolved Scottish Parliament. In 1999, after nearly three centuries, Scotland once again had its own legislative body, based at Holyrood in Edinburgh.

The new parliament was granted powers over health, education, transport, and justice. It also introduced distinctive policies such as free university tuition for Scottish students and free personal care for the elderly — measures that reflected a distinct social policy ethos.

The reestablishment of the parliament was celebrated as a democratic triumph. The opening ceremony, featuring a stirring poem by Edwin Morgan and the symbolic "Stone of Destiny" (temporarily returned from Westminster), underscored a proud reclaiming of Scottish political agency.

The 2014 Independence Referendum

The dream of full independence did not fade with devolution. Under the SNP, which gained a majority in 2011, the push for a new referendum gathered steam.

On September 18, 2014, Scotland held its most momentous vote in modern history. After months of passionate debate, voter turnout reached a staggering 85% — a testament to the deep emotional and political engagement of the Scottish people.

Ultimately, 55% voted to remain in the UK, while 45% voted for independence. The result was a profound moment of both heartbreak and renewed resolve for the independence movement. Despite the "No" vote, the referendum galvanized civic engagement and shifted the political landscape permanently.

Brexit and Renewed Calls for Independence

In 2016, the United Kingdom voted to leave the European Union, but Scotland overwhelmingly voted to remain (62%). This divergence reignited calls for a second independence referendum, as many Scots felt their democratic will had been ignored once again.

The SNP and other pro-independence voices argue that Brexit fundamentally alters the Union's nature and presents a new case for Scottish sovereignty. Whether or when a second referendum will take place remains a central, unresolved question in Scottish politics.

Independence: A Question of Heart and Mind

At its core, Scotland's independence debate is about more than economics or constitutional arrangements — it is about identity, belonging, and the right to choose one's own path.

Supporters of independence see it as a chance to shape a fairer, more progressive society, reconnect with Europe, and express Scotland's distinct cultural and historical values on the world stage. Opponents, meanwhile, emphasize economic stability, shared history, and the benefits of union.

The spirit of independence is not confined to politics. It pulses through art, music, and everyday conversation. It appears in murals on tenement walls, in poetry recited at ceilidhs, and in the quiet pride of small communities that cherish their right to self-determination.

The Future Unwritten

The story of Scottish independence remains a living, unfolding narrative. It is not merely a question to be answered in a single referendum but an ongoing conversation about who the Scots are and who they want to be.

From the echoing halls of Arbroath Abbey to the modern debating chamber at Holyrood, the Scottish people have continually returned to this question: How do we balance our fierce independence with the realities of a shared world?

Whether Scotland eventually stands as an independent nation or continues within the United Kingdom, the spirit that animates this debate — the belief in the right to decide — is among the nation's most cherished legacies.

Chapter 14: The Makers: Great Scots Who Changed the World

Scotland, though small in size, has given the world an astonishing number of thinkers, inventors, artists, and leaders who have forever changed the course of human history. From scientists who unlocked the secrets of the universe to poets who captured the soul of the common folk, these "Makers" embody Scotland's restless curiosity, creativity, and courage.

In this chapter, we meet some of the remarkable Scots who built bridges — both literal and metaphorical — to new worlds and new ideas. Their stories illuminate not just Scottish brilliance, but a shared human spirit striving to explore, understand, and create.

James Watt: Powering the Modern World

James Watt, born in Greenock in 1736, is often credited with sparking the Industrial Revolution. His improvements to the steam engine — including the crucial separate condenser — dramatically increased efficiency and made steam power a cornerstone of modern industry.

Watt's engines powered factories, revolutionized mining, and transformed transportation. By turning steam into a reliable source of power, Watt helped usher in an age of mass production and urbanization. His name lives on in the "watt," a standard unit of power that fuels our everyday lives, from lightbulbs to massive generators.

Alexander Fleming: The Accidental Savior

In 1928, Alexander Fleming, a modest Scottish biologist from Ayrshire, returned from vacation to find that a mold had killed the bacteria in one of his Petri dishes. That chance discovery led to penicillin — the first true antibiotic, which has since saved hundreds of millions of lives worldwide.

Fleming's humble observation reshaped medicine forever. Before penicillin, even minor infections could be fatal. His breakthrough turned the tide against bacterial diseases and laid the foundation for modern antibiotics.

Mary Somerville: The Queen of Science

Mary Somerville, born in 1780 in Jedburgh, was a self-taught mathematician and astronomer whose writings helped popularize and explain complex scientific ideas.

Her book *On the Connexion of the Physical Sciences* inspired the term "scientist" and played a crucial role in shaping 19th-century scientific thought. She championed women's education and became an icon of intellectual rigor and quiet perseverance in a male-dominated world.

Today, Somerville College at Oxford stands as a testament to her legacy, reminding us that intellectual brilliance knows no gender.

Adam Smith: The Father of Economics

Born in Kirkcaldy in 1723, Adam Smith is best known for *The Wealth of Nations*, the book that laid the foundations for modern economics.

Smith's ideas about free markets, division of labor, and the "invisible hand" remain deeply influential today. Yet, he was more than an economist; he was a moral philosopher who deeply believed in fairness and social welfare. His first book, *The Theory of Moral Sentiments*, explored human empathy and ethics, showing that Smith's vision of society was far richer than mere market transactions.

David Hume: The Skeptical Philosopher

A giant of the Scottish Enlightenment, David Hume challenged conventional wisdom about reason, religion, and human nature. His *Treatise of Human Nature* and essays on understanding and empiricism reshaped philosophy, influencing thinkers from Kant to Darwin.

Hume's radical skepticism questioned the certainty of everything from causality to religious belief. His clear, engaging prose made complex ideas accessible, earning him admirers and critics alike. Today, he is considered one of the greatest philosophers in Western history.

Robert Burns: The Voice of the People

No celebration of Scottish genius would be complete without Robert Burns, the national bard. Born in 1759 in Alloway, Burns wrote poems and songs in Scots dialect, giving voice to ordinary people's joys, struggles, and dreams.

His works, from "Auld Lang Syne" to "Tam o' Shanter," continue to unite Scots at home and abroad. Burns Night, celebrated every January 25th with whisky, haggis, and poetry, is a global testament to his enduring appeal.

Burns was a poet of the people, deeply democratic in spirit. His lines, "A man's a man for a' that," capture a timeless message of equality and human dignity.

Sir Walter Scott: The Romantic Novelist

Sir Walter Scott transformed historical fiction into a global literary phenomenon. His novels, including *Waverley*, *Rob Roy*, and *Ivanhoe*, captured Scotland's turbulent history and romantic landscapes, turning them into subjects of fascination worldwide.

Scott also played a crucial role in shaping modern perceptions of Scottish identity. His orchestration of King George IV's visit to Scotland in 1822 popularized tartan and Highland dress, cementing their status as national symbols.

John Logie Baird: The Father of Television

In 1926, John Logie Baird gave the first public demonstration of television in London. Born in Helensburgh in 1888, Baird's early experiments included using biscuit tins and tea chests to create his first devices.

Though often overshadowed by later technological advancements, Baird's pioneering work laid the foundation for the global broadcasting industry, forever changing how we communicate and experience the world.

Andrew Carnegie: The Industrialist and Philanthropist

Born into poverty in Dunfermline in 1835, Andrew Carnegie emigrated to America and became one of the richest men in history through the steel industry.

Yet Carnegie's legacy lies not just in his wealth but in his generosity. He gave away nearly 90% of his fortune, funding libraries, universities, and scientific research around the world. His belief in the "Gospel of Wealth" — that the rich have a moral obligation to distribute their wealth for the greater good — reshaped philanthropy.

Modern Makers

Scotland's tradition of innovation continues into the present. Figures like physicist Peter Higgs, who theorized the Higgs boson, and JK Rowling, who created the Harry Potter universe while living in Edinburgh, demonstrate that the Scottish creative spark remains bright.

Musicians like Annie Lennox and innovators in renewable energy, medicine, and artificial intelligence all carry forward this legacy of making — not just things, but ideas, stories, and a better future.

The Shared Spirit

Across centuries and continents, what unites these "Makers" is a shared spirit: a refusal to accept the world as it is and a relentless desire to improve, question, and create.

This spirit is deeply Scottish yet universally human. It speaks to something in all of us — the impulse to reach beyond our circumstances, to imagine new possibilities, and to leave something lasting for those who come after.

Inspiration for Tomorrow

As you walk through Scotland's cities today — past statues of philosophers in Edinburgh, engineering marvels in Glasgow, or quiet countryside memorials — you sense this inheritance. It's in the libraries funded by Carnegie, in the poetry of Burns recited by a schoolchild, and in the quiet pride of an engineer describing a new invention.

The story of Scotland's "Makers" is far from over. Every new thinker, artist, or dreamer who picks up a pen, a microscope, or a violin carries forward that torch. And in doing so, they ensure that Scotland's story is not merely a tale of the past but an ever-evolving celebration of what humanity can achieve.

Chapter 15: The Everlasting Flame: Scotland in the Modern World

As the sun dips below the horizon on a Highland loch, the last golden light glinting off the water, one cannot help but feel that Scotland is a land forever caught between past and present — a place where ancient echoes reverberate alongside the buzz of modern life.

Today, Scotland stands as a proud, dynamic nation, alive with contradictions and possibilities. It carries the weight of centuries yet strides forward with a spirit as fierce and fresh as the wind whipping through the glens. In this final chapter, we explore Scotland's place in the modern world and the enduring flame that lights its future.

A New Political Awakening

The reestablishment of the Scottish Parliament in 1999 marked a profound shift. After nearly three centuries, Scotland regained a legislative voice in Edinburgh, symbolizing not just political devolution but a renewed self-confidence.

Since then, Holyrood has charted its own course on many issues: offering free university tuition to Scottish students, pioneering climate change legislation, and emphasizing social welfare policies rooted in community values.

The independence referendum of 2014 and the ongoing debates around Brexit and EU membership have kept questions of sovereignty alive and vibrant. While Scots ultimately voted to stay in the UK in 2014, the narrow margin and subsequent political developments, including Brexit, have ensured that the spirit of self-determination remains a powerful current in national life.

These debates are not simply about borders or treaties; they are conversations about identity, values, and the type of society Scots want to build. They echo through village halls, city streets, and online forums — a testament to a deeply engaged and passionate populace.

Economic Reinvention

From shipyards and steel mills to financial services and renewable energy, Scotland has always adapted to economic tides. In recent decades, heavy industries that once defined the nation have given way to new sectors.

Edinburgh has become a global hub for finance and technology, known for its striking blend of medieval alleys and gleaming modern offices. Glasgow has reinvented itself as a center for culture and design, embracing its working-class heritage while looking forward with artistic and entrepreneurial energy.

Perhaps most striking is Scotland's leadership in renewable energy. The country has embraced wind, tidal, and hydroelectric power with gusto, aiming to become a world leader in green technology and achieve net-zero emissions by 2045. Offshore wind farms now dot the coastlines, their giant blades turning like futuristic sentinels over ancient seas.

The North Sea oil boom of the late 20th century, though controversial, also played a major role in Scotland's modern economic story, providing revenue and sparking debates about ownership and sustainability that continue today.

Cultural Renaissance

Scotland's cultural identity today is as vibrant as ever, shaped by tradition but open to the world. The arts have become a powerful expression of national spirit and diversity.

The Edinburgh Festival Fringe, the world's largest arts festival, draws performers and audiences from across the globe, turning the historic city into a kaleidoscope of creativity each August. Musicians continue to blend folk traditions with contemporary styles, from fiddle-driven indie rock to Gaelic hip-hop.

Scottish literature enjoys global acclaim, with writers like Irvine Welsh and Ali Smith pushing boundaries and capturing the complexities of modern Scottish life. Filmmakers bring both raw realism and dreamy romanticism to screens big and small, showcasing Scotland's landscapes and its people's stories to the world.

Meanwhile, a younger generation of Scots embraces their Gaelic and Scots languages as living, evolving parts of their identity. Language revival efforts, from community classes to bilingual schools, signal a new pride and curiosity about Scotland's linguistic heritage.

A Tapestry of Peoples

Modern Scotland is a mosaic of communities. Waves of immigration from South Asia, Africa, Eastern Europe, and beyond have enriched the cultural landscape. Scottish identity has expanded beyond ancestry and clan to embrace anyone who shares in its communal spirit.

Cities now hum with diverse languages and cuisines; mosques, gurdwaras, and churches stand side by side. Festivals celebrating Diwali, Eid, and Chinese New Year flourish alongside Hogmanay and Burns Night, creating a cultural vibrancy that feels both local and global.

This inclusive Scotland still wrestles with challenges — from racism and economic inequality to debates over integration and belonging — but the direction is clear: an evolving identity that honors the past while welcoming the future.

Reconnecting with Nature

Perhaps nowhere is the Scottish spirit more evident than in its landscapes. In recent decades, there has been a powerful movement toward rewilding and environmental stewardship.

Projects to restore native woodlands, reintroduce lost species like the beaver, and protect marine ecosystems represent a deepening respect for the land and its rhythms. Outdoor activities, from hillwalking to wild swimming, have seen a resurgence, as Scots and visitors alike seek to reconnect with the natural world.

The old stories live on in these wild spaces. Every glen, loch, and moor feels imbued with myth, as if the spirits of ancient clans and storytellers still walk beside you, whispering secrets in the wind.

Global Connections

Scotland's diaspora remains strong and engaged. Millions of people around the world — from Nova Scotia to Dunedin — proudly trace their roots back to the misty glens and bustling cities of Scotland.

Diaspora networks foster cultural exchange and keep traditions alive abroad, while also supporting economic and academic links back to Scotland. Tartan Day in North America, Highland games in New Zealand, and Burns suppers in South Africa are just a few examples of how Scots abroad keep the flame alive.

Scotland's influence on global culture is profound: from whisky to golf, from bagpipes to cutting-edge science, the mark of this small nation echoes far beyond its borders.

The Flame Endures

As we reach the end of our journey through Scotland's story, we see a nation in constant motion — grounded in fierce pride yet unafraid to change.

Scotland today stands as a beacon of resilience and creativity, forever balancing the pull of tradition with the push of innovation. Whether navigating questions of independence, forging new paths in renewable energy, or redefining what it means to be Scottish in a diverse world, the people carry forward the spirit of the Declaration of Arbroath: the fierce belief in the right to choose their own destiny.

In every ceilidh dance, in every echo of a piper's lament on a city street, in every handfasting ribbon tied on a windswept hill, the everlasting flame burns on.

An Invitation

Scotland's story does not belong to Scots alone. It is an invitation — to dreamers, thinkers, wanderers, and makers everywhere. It calls to those who long to stand on the edge of a loch at dawn and feel history in the mist, to those who value community and courage, to those who believe in the power of story to shape the future.

Whether your ancestors sailed from these shores or you simply feel a tug at your heart when you see a tartan or hear a fiddle tune, you are part of this unfolding story.

So come, walk these ancient paths, share a dram, listen to the old songs, and add your own verse to the ballad that is Scotland.

Bibliography

Primary Historical Sources

- The Declaration of Arbroath, 1320. National Records of Scotland.
- Acts of Union, 1707. The UK National Archives.
- The Treaty of Edinburgh-Northampton, 1328. British Library Collections.
- The Scottish National Covenant, 1638. Church of Scotland Records.

Books and Monographs

- Devine, T. M. *The Scottish Nation: A Modern History*. London: Penguin Books, 2000.
- Smout, T. C. *A History of the Scottish People, 1560–1830*. London: Fontana Press, 1969.
- Lynch, Michael. *Scotland: A New History*. London: Pimlico, 1992.
- Maclean, Fitzroy. *A Concise History of Scotland*. London: Thames & Hudson, 1993.
- Magnusson, Magnus. *Scotland: The Story of a Nation*. New York: Grove Press, 2000.
- Prebble, John. *Culloden*. London: Secker & Warburg, 1961.
- Mitchison, Rosalind. *A History of Scotland*. London: Routledge, 2002.
- Brown, Michael. *The Wars of Scotland, 1214–1371*. Edinburgh: Edinburgh University Press, 2004.
- Herman, Arthur. *How the Scots Invented the Modern World*. New York: Crown Publishing, 2001.
- Pittock, Murray. *The Myth of the Jacobite Clans: The Jacobite Army in 1745*. Edinburgh: Edinburgh University Press, 2009.

Articles and Essays

- Kidd, Colin. "The Scottish Enlightenment and the Highlands." *Journal of Scottish Historical Studies*, Vol. 24, No. 1 (2004).

- Bowie, Karin. "Scottish Public Opinion and the Making of the Union of 1707." *The Scottish Historical Review*, Vol. 86, No. 2 (2007).
- Fry, Michael. "Scotland and the British Empire." *Transactions of the Royal Historical Society*, Vol. 13 (2003).

Cultural and Diaspora Studies

- Harper, Marjory, and Stephen Constantine. *Migration and Empire*. Oxford: Oxford University Press, 2010.
- Bumsted, J. M. *The People's Clearance: Highland Emigration to British North America, 1770–1815*. Edinburgh: Edinburgh University Press, 1982.
- McCarthy, Angela. *Personal Narratives of Irish and Scottish Migration, 1921–65: For Spirit and Adventure*. Manchester: Manchester University Press, 2007.

Literary Sources

- Burns, Robert. *Poems and Songs*. Various collected editions.
- Scott, Walter. *Waverley* and other novels. Edinburgh: Archibald Constable, 1814 onward.
- MacDiarmid, Hugh. *A Drunk Man Looks at the Thistle*. Edinburgh: The Porpoise Press, 1926.

Museums and Heritage Collections

- National Museum of Scotland Collections and Digital Archives.
- Scottish National Gallery and Library, Historical Manuscripts.
- Glasgow Museums Resource Centre.
- Highland Folk Museum Archives.

Online and Multimedia Resources

- BBC Scotland History Archives.
- National Library of Scotland Digital Collections.
- Scottish Government Publications on Independence and Devolution.

- Historic Environment Scotland, official guides and online exhibitions.
- The University of Edinburgh, Scottish Studies Online Resources.

Acknowledgment

This bibliography reflects a blend of academic works, primary sources, and publicly accessible archives that together illuminate the rich, complex story of Scotland — from ancient roots to modern debates. It honors the contributions of countless historians, poets, chroniclers, and communities who have kept Scotland's story alive across generations.

Further Reading

For those inspired to wander deeper into Scotland's story, here is a selection of accessible and beautifully written books that bring Scottish history, culture, and spirit vividly to life. These works blend storytelling with scholarship and are perfect for anyone — whether you're a curious beginner or a seasoned Scotophile.

General History and Culture

- **Neil Oliver, *A History of Scotland***
  A highly engaging overview by the popular historian and TV presenter, covering everything from prehistoric times to the present day with warmth and clarity.
- **Alistair Moffat, *Scotland: A History from Earliest Times***
  A sweeping narrative that beautifully captures the grand arcs and small details that make Scotland's story so compelling.
- **James Hunter, *The Making of the Crofting Community***
  An insightful look at the Highland Clearances and the enduring spirit of crofting culture.

Scottish Diaspora and Global Influence

- **Tom Devine,** *To the Ends of the Earth: Scotland's Global Diaspora, 1750–2010*
  A fascinating exploration of how Scots carried their culture and values across the globe.
- **Angela McCarthy,** *Scotland's Diaspora: History of Scottish Emigration and Emigrants*
  Rich personal stories and historical analysis of Scottish communities around the world.

Biography and Personal Stories

- **Herman, Arthur,** *How the Scots Invented the Modern World*
  A lively, thought-provoking look at how Scottish thinkers and innovators shaped modern society far beyond their borders.
- **Robert Crawford,** *Scotland's Books: A History of Scottish Literature*
  A delightful journey through Scotland's literary tradition, from medieval ballads to contemporary novels.

Myth, Folklore, and Cultural Traditions

- **Lizanne Henderson and Edward J. Cowan,** *Scottish Fairy Belief: A History*
  A fascinating dive into Scotland's rich folklore traditions and the deep roots of its mythical creatures and stories.
- **Alexander McCall Smith,** *Scotland: The Autobiography*
  A unique book that weaves together diaries, letters, and memoirs from Scots over centuries, creating a collective "voice" of the nation.

Highlands, Clans, and Landscape

- **John Prebble,** *Culloden*
  A vivid and dramatic account of the last battle fought on British soil and its profound consequences for the Highlands.
- **Patrick Baker,** *The Unremembered Places: Exploring Scotland's Wild Histories*
  An evocative exploration of hidden historical sites in Scotland's most remote landscapes.

Contemporary Scotland

- **Alistair Darling,** *Back from the Brink: 1,000 Days at Number 11*
  A candid look at recent economic and political challenges, including perspectives on Scotland's place in the UK.
- **Murray Pittock,** *Scotland: The Global History, 1603 to the Present*
  An excellent overview connecting Scotland's history to its modern global identity.

Fiction to Capture the Spirit

- **Lewis Grassic Gibbon,** *Sunset Song*
  A lyrical novel that beautifully captures the changes in rural Scotland during the early 20th century.
- **Ali Smith,** *There but for the*
  A witty, inventive modern novel by one of Scotland's most celebrated contemporary authors.

An Invitation

These books invite you to climb higher into Scotland's mountains of history, swim deeper into its lochs of story, and walk further into its forests of tradition.

No matter where you begin, each page is another step into a land where the past and present dance together — and where your own story might find an echo among the heather.

Glossary

Act of Union (1707)

The agreement that unified the Scottish and English Parliaments to create the Kingdom of Great Britain. It dissolved Scotland's independent parliament but allowed Scotland to maintain its own legal and educational systems.

Bagpipes

A traditional wind instrument associated with Scotland, particularly the Highlands. Known for its haunting, powerful sound, it became a symbol of Scottish identity and martial spirit.

Caber Toss

A traditional event in Highland Games where athletes toss a tall, heavy wooden pole (the caber) end over end, requiring strength and balance.

Ceilidh (pronounced "kay-lee")

A social gathering featuring music, dance, storytelling, and Gaelic folk traditions. Ceilidhs are joyful celebrations of community and culture.

Clan

A kinship-based social structure central to Highland society, where members claim descent from a common ancestor and follow a chief. Clans are often associated with particular tartans and territories.

Covenanters

17th-century Scottish Presbyterians who signed covenants pledging to maintain their religious freedoms and resist attempts to impose Anglican worship practices.

Declaration of Arbroath

A 1320 letter sent to the Pope asserting Scotland's independence from England and affirming the sovereignty of the Scottish people.

Diaspora

The scattering of Scots around the world, particularly during the 18th and 19th centuries, creating vibrant communities abroad, from Canada to Australia.

Gaelic (Scottish Gaelic)

A Celtic language historically spoken in the Highlands and Islands of Scotland. Efforts are ongoing today to revive and preserve it.

Highlands

The mountainous, northern region of Scotland known for its dramatic landscapes, clan history, and Gaelic cultural traditions.

Jacobite

Supporters of the exiled Stuart royal family who sought to restore them to the British throne during a series of uprisings in the 17th and 18th centuries.

Kirk

The national church of Scotland, which is Presbyterian in governance. The word "kirk" is the Scots term for "church."

Loch

The Scots Gaelic word for "lake" or "sea inlet." Scotland has many famous lochs, including Loch Ness and Loch Lomond.

Lowlands

The southern and eastern parts of Scotland characterized by gentler terrain and historically more Anglicized culture. Distinct from the Gaelic traditions of the Highlands.

Massacre of Glencoe

A tragic 1692 event when government forces killed members of Clan MacDonald in their homes after they had offered them hospitality. It remains a symbol of betrayal in Scottish memory.

Picts

An ancient people who lived in what is now eastern and northern Scotland during the Late Iron Age and Early Medieval periods. Known for their mysterious symbol stones and fierce resistance to Roman conquest.

Reformation

The 16th-century religious movement that transformed Scotland from a Catholic country to a predominantly Protestant one, establishing the Presbyterian Kirk.

Schiltron

A dense formation of spearmen used effectively by Scottish forces, especially at battles like Bannockburn, to repel cavalry charges.

Sgian-dubh

A small, single-edged knife traditionally worn tucked into the top of a kilt hose (sock). Part of formal Highland dress.

Stone of Destiny

An ancient symbol of Scottish monarchy, used for the coronation of kings at Scone Abbey. It was taken to England in 1296 and returned to Scotland in 1996 (though now kept in Edinburgh Castle).

Tartan

A patterned cloth of criss-crossed horizontal and vertical bands in multiple colors. Each clan has its own tartan pattern, and tartan is a symbol of Scottish heritage worldwide.

Thistle

Scotland's national emblem. Legend says an invading Norse army was thwarted when one of their soldiers stepped on a thistle, alerting Scots to the attack.

Union of the Crowns (1603)

When James VI of Scotland inherited the English throne as James I, uniting the two crowns under one monarch but keeping separate parliaments and legal systems.

Whisky (Uisge Beatha)

Scotland's national drink, distilled from malted barley and water, often simply called "Scotch." The Gaelic term *uisge beatha* means "water of life."

A Note to the Reader

This glossary is here to help you feel at home in Scotland's story. If you come across a word that feels foreign or mysterious, remember: every term carries with it centuries of songs, battles, gatherings, and quiet evenings by the hearth.

Timeline of Major Events

Prehistoric & Early Medieval

1. **c. 10,000 BC** — First human settlements in Scotland after the last Ice Age.
2. **c. 3000 BC** — Construction of Neolithic sites like Skara Brae and stone circles.
3. **c. AD 297** — First mention of the Picts by Roman chroniclers.
4. **c. 500** — Arrival of the Gaels from Ireland; formation of Dál Riata.
5. **843** — Kenneth MacAlpin traditionally unites Picts and Gaels to form Alba.

Medieval

1. **1034** — Duncan I becomes first king of a unified "Scotland."
2. **1296** — Edward I invades; beginning of the Wars of Independence.
3. **1297** — William Wallace defeats the English at Stirling Bridge.
4. **1306** — Robert the Bruce crowned King of Scots.
5. **1314** — Battle of Bannockburn; major Scottish victory.
6. **1320** — Declaration of Arbroath asserts Scottish independence.
7. **1328** — Treaty of Edinburgh-Northampton recognizes Scotland's independence.

Early Modern

1. **1603** — Union of the Crowns: James VI of Scotland becomes James I of England.
2. **1707** — Act of Union joins Scottish and English parliaments.
3. **1715 & 1745** — Jacobite risings attempt to restore Stuart monarchy.
4. **1746** — Battle of Culloden; final defeat of Jacobite forces.
5. **1782** — Repeal of the Dress Act; tartan and Highland dress revived.

Industrial and Modern

1. **1800s** — Highland Clearances force mass emigration and reshape land ownership.
2. **1822** — King George IV's visit to Scotland, orchestrated by Sir Walter Scott, popularizes tartan.
3. **1843** — The "Disruption" splits the Church of Scotland; Free Church founded.
4. **1928** — Alexander Fleming discovers penicillin.
5. **1945–1970s** — Postwar industrial decline; North Sea oil boom begins.
6. **1997** — Referendum supports creation of a devolved Scottish Parliament.
7. **1999** — Opening of the modern Scottish Parliament at Holyrood.
8. **2014** — Independence referendum; 55% vote to remain in the UK.
9. **2016** — Brexit vote; Scotland votes 62% to remain in the EU.
10. **2020s** — Ongoing debates over independence and Scotland's future in Europe.

A Note on the Journey

This timeline and illustration guide are designed to help you follow Scotland's story visually and chronologically, connecting the sweeping narrative of centuries to the personal experiences and cultural symbols that make this nation unforgettable.

www.ingramcontent.com/pod-product-compliance
Lightning Source LLC
Chambersburg PA
CBHW060817050426
42449CB00008B/1705